D1297399

D CONVENT
ST. LOUIS
PROVINCIAL LIBRARY

A7

232.931
G33/M37

The Spiritual Maternity According to
Saint Louis Mary De Montfort

701

Mary's Spiritual Maternity

according to St. Louis de Montfort

Patrick Gaffney, S.M.M.

MONTFORT PUBLICATIONS
Bay Shore, New York

IMPRIMI POTEST

Very Rev. Leo Blais, S.M.M.
Provincial Superior

NIHIL OBSTAT

Rev. Msgr. John T. Byrne, Ph.D.
Censor Deputatus
March 18, 1976

IMPRIMATUR

John J. Cardinal Carberry
Archbishop of Saint Louis
March 25, 1976

CONTENTS

PART II THE PREMISES FROM WHICH MONTFORT DEDUCES THE SPIRITUAL MATERNITY

ABBREVIATIONS

AAS   —Acta Apostolicae Sedis

ASS   —Acta Sanctae Sedis

BEM   —Bulletin de la Societé Française d'Études Mariales

Cantiques —Les Cantiques du Bienheureux de Montfort (The Hymns of Saint Louis de Montfort, unpublished in English)

Lettres   —Les Lettres du Bienheureux de Montfort (The Letters of Saint Louis de Montfort, unpublished in English)

P.G.   —Patrologiae Cursus Completus, Series Prima (Patrologia Graeca), Editio Migne.

P.L.   —Patrologiae Cursus Completus, Series Secunda (Patrologia Latina) Editio Migne.

Sagesse   —L'Amour de la Sagesse Éternelle The Love of the Eternal Wisdom by Saint Louis de Montfort

Secret   —Le Secret de Marie The Secret of Mary by Saint Louis de Montfort

V.Dév.   —Le Traité de la Vraie Dévotion à la Très Sainte Vierge The True Devotion to the Blessed Virgin by Saint Louis de Montfort

Other abbreviations are self-evident.

The excellent critical edition of Montfort's works, *Oeuvres complètes de saint Louis-Marie Grignion de Montfort* (Complete works of Saint Louis de Montfort), (Paris, 1966), omits some of Montfort's *Cantiques* and also sections of both the *Cahier de Sermons* (*Sermon Notebook*) and the *Cahier de Notes* (*Notebook*). We have, therefore, quoted from other editions of Saint Louis' works, listed in the bibliography.

To an outstanding Marian Prelate
John Joseph Cardinal Carberry,
Archbishop of Saint Louis,
whose coat-of-arms is emblazoned
with the motto,

MARY,
QUEEN
AND
MOTHER

AUTHOR'S PREFACE

Especially since his canonization in 1947, theologians have scrutinized the writings of Saint Louis Mary Grignion de Montfort (1673-1716). His present influence upon the Christian world, primarily because of his masterpiece on Our Lady, *The True Devotion to the Blessed Virgin,* is difficult to measure; there is no doubt that his writings have played and continue to play an important role in the life of the Church.

Saint Louis' works have always been recognized by the Church as authentic teachings, founded upon the rock of sound theology. Primarily because his principal Marian manuscript (erroneously called *The True Devotion* by the first publishers) was only discovered in 1842, little was done to sound the true depths of these foundations until the latter part of the last century. His *True Devotion,* translated into English by Father Faber in 1862, was discussed, at least in part, by Cardinal Newman and E. B. Pusey and also influenced the Marian poetry of Gerard Manley Hopkins. All of Montfort's writings were examined thoroughly by Roman theologians in view of his beatification which occurred in 1888. Nonetheless, it is only in this century and especially since his canonization, that theologians have attempted to show the richness and exactness of the doctrine of this one time almost forgotten missionary. Many theologians, bishops, and Popes have joined in the praise of this vagabond priest who roamed the countryside of Western France during the reign of *Le Roi Soleil,* attempting to renew the faith of the people.

A. Lhoumeau, H. Gebhard, Cardinal Mercier, G. Roschini, E. Mura, R. Garrigou-Lagrange, O.P., G. Philips are only some of the scholars who have been fascinated by the simplicity and yet solidity of the works of Saint Louis de Montfort.

However, much remains to be done, especially in this post Vatican II age. The missionary's writings have to be examined in the light of the documents of the Second Vatican Council and his Marian teaching studied in view of recent developments in Mariology and the Apostolic Exhortation of Pope Paul VI, *Marialis Cultus* and the Pastoral Letter of the American Bishops on Mary, *Behold Your Mother*. In light of these documents, this short work attempts to delve into the foundations of the spiritual maternity as taught by Saint Louis de Montfort. This aspect of the saint's Mariology was chosen for special study, not only because of Pope Paul's predilection for the title Mother of the Church, but also because one of the barriers keeping so many back from accepting the doctrine of Saint Louis is a misunderstanding of his expressions *"slave," "slavery," "Queen," "Mistress."* Some would believe that Montfort has forgotten that Mary is our Mother and that he regards Our Lady more as an austere, forbidding Empress to whom we, as servile slaves, must subject ourselves. Nothing could be further from the truth. It is in the hope of clarifying Montfort's teaching on the spiritual maternity that we offer this overview of the foundations of this Marian prerogative according to the doctrine of Saint Louis Mary de Montfort.

INTRODUCTION

"Having read nearly all the books which profess to treat of devotion to Our Lady and having conversed familiarly with the best and wisest men of these latter times . . .";[1] such is the claim of Saint Louis de Montfort. And although at the time of the writing of the *True Devotion to the Blessed Virgin,* the works treating of Our Lady did not number the over 100,000 which R. Laurentin declares existed even twenty-five years ago,[2] nonetheless, Saint Louis' statement does cover a vast field. We do know from his *Notebook* that he had consulted not only Scripture and the Fathers of the Church, but also Suarez, Olier, Poiré, de Bérulle, Boudon, Camus, Crasset, St. Jure and so many others. His friendship with the Dominicans, the Sulpicians and the Jesuits, his pilgrimage to Rome, all gave him the opportunity to "converse familiarly" with some of the greatest theologians of his time. This deep study, coupled with his special mystical gifts, gave him an excellent grasp of Mary's role in salvation history, as it was understood in his day. And this profound knowledge of the role of Mary certainly included one of her most illustrious privileges, the spiritual maternity.

At the time of Saint Louis, it must be remembered, the doctrine of the spiritual maternity was already developed. Although not brought out explicitly until the end of the fourth century, nonetheless, the truth behind the term "Mother of Men" was firmly established in the famous theory of the *'recapitulatio'* of Saint Justin[3] and of Saint Ireneus.[4] Origen, basing himself on the identification of a Christian with Christ, had already applied

to others than Jesus the state of being children of Mary.[5]
Saint Epiphanius, reasoning from the Divine Maternity, appears to be the first to call Mary "Mother of the
Living."[6] From Saint Augustine's disputed text: "Mary
is mother indeed in spirit, not of our Head, which is
the Savior Himself ... but clearly she is the mother of
His members,"[7] succeeding generations have taken the
argument for Mary's motherhood of men from the unity
of Head and members of the Mystical Body.

During this era, however, and up until the 12th century,
it is more the function of Mary's motherhood rather than
the motherhood itself that found expression in the writings of the Fathers, as is seen in the titles which Saint
Germain of Constantinople gives Our Lady: "the solace
of Christians," "refuge of sinners."[8] With Saint An-
selm, however, "a new era opens in which all reserve is
cast aside and Mary is fondly and regularly addressed as
our Mother."[9] From the Divine Maternity, Saint An-
selm concluded to Mary's Motherhood of men, calling her
"mater rerum recreatarum."[10] Although Saint Bernard,
at least in his writings, never addressed Mary as "My
Mother," the doctrine of the spiritual maternity is to
be found in his homilies[11] and clearly expressed by his
followers.[12] Rupert of Deutz, having drawn the fact of
Mary's motherhood of men from the mystery of the Incarnation, sees this privilege also in the *"Ecce Mater
Tua."*[13] Pseudo-Albert the Great went a step further
and explicitly taught Mary's spiritual maternity reasoning
from her cooperation with Christ in the work of our Redemption.[14]

Saint Thomas, although he too, never addressed Mary
as "Our Mother" in his writings,[15] implicitly provided
us with theological arguments for this mystical maternity
of Mary.[16] His friend, Saint Bonaventure, clearly expressed this prerogative of Mary.[17] Arguing from the
Incarnation and the words of Christ on the Cross, Saint
Bernardine concluded to a true maternity of grace in our

regard.[18] Saint Louis de Montfort could therefore find the spiritual maternity well grounded in the tradition of the Church.

However, the writings of the Fathers and mediaeval theologians are not the immediate sources for Montfort's doctrine on the spiritual maternity. His knowledge of the teaching of tradition and his study of this prerogative of Mary were taken, for the most part, not directly from the sources themselves, but from the theologians and spiritual writers of his own century. To the French School of spirituality, especially to Cardinal de Bérulle and Jean Jacques Olier, Montfort owes much of his insights into the spiritual maternity.[19] However, among the principal sources of the missionary for his teaching on this prerogative of Our Lady are also J. Crasset,[20] L. D'Argentan[21] and F. Poiré.[22]

These were the sources for Saint Louis' teachings concerning the spiritual maternity. How he made use of this material will be seen in this work; but we shall never fully grasp Montfort's explanation of the foundations of Mary's Motherhood of men if we do not, first of all, understand the nature of Saint Louis' vocation.

Saint Louis de Montfort is not a professional theologian; he is primarily a missionary. From the early days of his priesthood we find his burning desire to preach the gospel to the poor. And when he saw that this wish was being thwarted, he did not hesitate to write to his spiritual director: "I had wished . . . to form myself for the Missions, and in particular for teaching catechism to the poor. . . . I feel a great desire to make Our Lord and His Holy Mother loved and to go about in a poor and simple way, catechizing the poor country people."[23] This ardent desire of Saint Louis was realized, for having been declared a Missionary Apostolic by Pope Clement XI himself, his life was spent going from town to town in Western France crushing the Jansenist heresy by his missions and retreats.

Not only his life proves to us that Montfort is primarily

a missionary, but his writings as well. His purpose is not
to write a manual of Mariology but, as he tells us himself:
"I speak particularly to the poor and simple, who being
of good will and having more faith than the common run
of scholars, believe more simply and more meritoriously.
I content myself with stating the truth quite plainly."[24]
He tells us that his *True Devotion* is nothing more than
what he has been preaching in all his missions.[25] Saint
Louis is primarily a missionary. His rostrum was the
pulpit; the crowded church, his class. We cannot then
expect to find in his writings a section devoted to proving
scholastically that Mary is our Mother, arranged as a question of the *Summa* of Saint Thomas.

However, Montfort is also a theologian. True, not in
the sense of someone who has composed a manual of theology or spent his life teaching systematic theology in a
university. However, if these were the requirements to
merit the title 'theologian,' with what right would the
Church declare Saint John of the Cross a Doctor of the
Church? Saint Louis de Montfort is a theologian, for his
writings, the fruit of his contemplation of God's Love, are
evidently founded upon the rock of theological truth, which
he is at pains to put into ordinary language for the simple
people of his time. His authority in the field of Mariology
has been recognized by Popes and theologians.[26]

The hermeneutical problems involved in trying to eluci-
date the writings of a contemplative missionary are evidently great and at times insurmountable. We have attempted to be completely objective in this study, not being
overly influenced by any personal or modern opinions, but
to discover the mind of Saint Louis on the question. We
have therefore, included *all* the works of the missionary in
our research. Undoubtedly, the most important writings
of Saint Louis concerning Our Lady are his *Traité de la
Vraie Dévotion à la Très Sainte Vierge* (The True Devotion to the Blessed Virgin)[27] and *Le Secret de Marie*
(The Secret of Mary).[28] However, we have also included

in the research all his other major works: *Le Secret Admirable du Très Saint Rosaire* (The Secret of the Rosary),[29] *L'Amour de la Sagesse Éternelle* (Love of the Eternal Wisdom),[30] *Lettre Circulaire aux amis de la Croix* (Circular Letter to the Friends of the Cross),[31] *Pour bien mourir* (Preparation for a Happy Death),[32] *Prière pour demander des Missionaires de la Compagnie de Marie* (Prayer for Missionaries),[33] *Allocution aux Associés de la Compagnie de Marie* (Allocution to the Associates of the Company of Mary),[34] *Règle des Filles de la Sagesse* (Rule of the Daughters of Wisdom),[35] *Règle de la Compagnie de Marie* (Rule of the Company of Mary),[36] *Cahier de Notes* (St. Louis' Notebook),[37] *Cahier des Sermons* (Notebook of Sermons),[38] his *Lettres*[39] and finally his volume of *Cantiques*,[40] written not so much for the rhyme but to teach the truths of the faith.[41]

In order to secure the objectivity desired, we have quoted from these works of Saint Louis continually, at times at length, including the original text in the footnotes, except when it concerns a non-controversial phrase. When citing the Cantiques, however, we have omitted its stanza form in an effort to shorten the already heavy notes.

In studying the spiritual maternity in these works of Saint Louis, we have limited ourselves to three main points: the fact of the spiritual maternity, the premises from which he deduces this prerogative and some explicitations of the nature of the spiritual maternity. Concerning the fact of the spiritual maternity we have included a study of the spiritual maternities in the life of Saint Louis, which not only reveals his continual insistence on this prerogative of Mary, but also may serve somewhat as an historical introduction to the general outlines of his life. In the second section, on the premises from which Montfort deduces this prerogative of Mary, we have followed a division which may be termed Montfort's own, considering the Will of the Father, the Son and the Holy Spirit. The third part of this study, "Some Explicitations on the

Nature of the Spiritual Maternity," will be published later, for we hope to make a critical study of this important facet in the light of Vatican Council II and recent theological opinions. From the chapters included in this publication, the reader can already have an insight into the general stance of Saint Louis de Montfort on the nature of this prerogative of Mary.

We hope that this short work will fill a need of many to understand the role of Our Lady in their lives. As R. Panikkar, the renowned expert on the relationship of Christianity to other religions, declared: "All is important: theology, science, culture, progress; all is very important; but without Mary our Christian life is mutilated and no matter how we try, without Mary we give a false impression of Christianity."[42] The understanding of Saint Louis de Montfort of Mary's place in salvation history —insights which Pope Pius XII called *"flagrans, solida ac recta"*[43]—still retain a beauty and power which make him stand out in the history of Christian spirituality. His explanation of the foundations of the spiritual maternity of Our Lady should help to clarify some of the questions posed today concerning devotion to Mary, especially consecration to her.

The words of Pope Paul VI aptly summarize our intention: "Thus our own time, faithfully attentive to tradition and to the progress of theology and the sciences, will make its contribution of praise to her whom, according to her own prophetical words, all generations will call blessed (cf. Lk 1:48)."[44]

PART ONE

The Fact of the Spiritual Maternity

Chapter One

The Fact of the Spiritual Maternity in the Life of St. Louis De Montfort

Understanding the spiritual maternity in its general sense of Mary cooperating in our birth to life in Christ, we will first of all show St. Louis de Montfort's insistence on the fact of this prerogative of Mary and then in the second part investigate the "proofs" which he gives for the spiritual maternity. We hope thereby to give some insight into the foundations upon which the saint builds his doctrine of the spiritual maternity.

In order to show Montfort's constant repetition of the *fact* that Mary is our spiritual Mother, we will first of all examine his life, and secondly, his writings.

The life of this "Master of Spirituality"[1] is relatively short: 43 years. However, as we learn from his numerous biographies, we may say that there are two main chapters to this saint's life, his years preceding the priesthood (1673-1700) and from his ordination to his death (1700-1716). This is not the place for a detailed biography of Saint Louis; we will merely point out various episodes in both sections of his life to prove his constant acknowledgement of the fact of Mary's spiritual maternity.

A. THE YEARS PRECEDING HIS PRIESTHOOD (1673-1700)

In the same year that Adam Widenfelt published at Gand his Jansenistic "Salutary advice of the Blessed Vir-

3

gin to Her Indiscreet Devotees,"[2] Louis Grignion was born at Montfort-la-Cane, Brittany, France: January 31, 1673. His intense devotion to Our Lady for which it was said of him "no one was so like Saint Bernard,"[3] is known to all who are the least bit acquainted with his life. But what is not so well known is that this devotion, this "promptitude of the will"[4] in relation to Mary had for its foundation, the spiritual maternity.

Our principal source for the early life of Saint Louis is his close friend, John Baptist Blain, who shortly after the saint's death wrote a summary of the life of Father de Montfort.[5] This confidant of Saint Louis (and also of St. John Baptist de la Salle), who knew him better than any other person of his lifetime, tells us that when Louis was a child, his love for Our Lady "was not something passing as it is in so many other children; it was constant."[6] And then Blain gives this important note on the quality of this devotion toward the Mother of God: "Everyone knows that he did not call Mary anything but 'his Mother, his good Mother, his dear Mother.' "[7] If, as Saint Thomas tells us, words are the signs of things understood,[8] we can well conclude that Montfort's attitude towards Our Lady was one of a child, for according to his biographers, the appellation 'my mother' was constantly in his conversation.

This filial love for Mary proved itself in action. "From his tender youth, he went to her with childlike simplicity, asking her for all his temporal and spiritual needs...; he was so assured because of the great confidence that he had in her goodness, of receiving them, that never did doubts or worry or perplexity hamper him. Everything, so he said, was done, once he had prayed to 'his good mother.' "[9] Montfort's love for Mary was then, filial; filial to an extraordinary degree, for all who were acquainted with him knew that he regarded Mary as his Mother and it was only as 'Mother' that he spoke of her, only as a child that he acted towards her.

This love for 'his good mother' never seemed to dwindle. Being the oldest living child, young Louis, while still a student of the Jesuits at Rennes, undertook the obligation of instructing his two younger brothers. We can get a glimpse of the manner he spoke about Our Lady from a letter written some years later: "Tell my brother Joseph . . . that he should place his studies in the hands of his good Mother, the Blessed Virgin."[10] Already he was teaching others his childlike devotion for Mary.

His biographers testify to this filial love for the Blessed Virgin during his student days at Rennes: "With the confidence of a well beloved child, he did nothing without consulting his Mother in heaven with affectionate prayers. At the feet of her statues, he prayed to her, he honored her, asked her protection, dedicated to her his innocence, consecrated himself to her service."[11] By the actions of young Louis Mary, we can legitimately conclude to his filial attitude towards the Mother of God, a quality which he never lost but rather perfected with the succeeding years.

Having decided to go to Paris to continue his education, in 1693 Saint Louis set out for his new life. He was leaving behind him his family, becoming what he would ask of his future missionaries of the Company of Mary: "detached from all things, without father, without mother, without brothers, without relatives according to the flesh, without friends according to the world."[12] No sooner does he lose sight of the city of Rennes, than he gives away his money, trades his clothes for the rags of a beggar so that he can live entirely on divine providence. Living thus only on the mercy of God, how strongly Montfort must have been drawn to a filial attitude towards God and Our Lady, such as he himself will later sing in one of his hymns on divine providence: "The Lord is my good Father, Jesus is my dear Savior, Mary is my good Mother; could I have greater joy!"[13] This spirit of separation from earthly things and of dependence on providence grew so much during his life that one day he would write to his parents:

"my father and my mother are in heaven."[14] Who has God for his Father must have Mary for his Mother, Montfort would declare in his *True Devotion*;[15] how true it must have been for Saint Louis himself.

After two years at the Sorbonne where he retained his habit of referring to Mary as 'my good Mother,'[16] Montfort entered St. Sulpice. It was here that he became acquainted with H. Boudon's *The Holy Slavery of the Admirable Mother of God,* and so influenced was he by it that we can find the substance of it in his *True Devotion to Mary*. At St. Sulpice, he read as much as possible on the "Holy Slavery" and founded a chapter of the confraternity of the Holy Slavery of Jesus in Mary. Many, deceived by the apparent meaning of the words 'slavery' and 'slave,' might think that Saint Louis is beginning to develop a cold reverence for Our Lady, since he considers himself as her 'slave.' Such a conclusion would be contrary not only to Saint Louis' notion of Holy Slavery[17] but also to the facts of his life; for in all events related of him at this time, in the letter we possess written during this period, there is but one constant reference to Mary: "my good Mother."[18]

While at St. Sulpice, Saint Louis was named librarian. The task was a welcome one, for it gave him the opportunity to become acquainted with many works on Our Lady. During this time he began to compile a notebook of various texts from different authors, principally about the Mother of God.[19] This *Notebook* does not necessarily express the opinions of the saint; he gathered quotations on Our Blessed Mother which interested him, primarily concerning disputed questions raised in part by Widenfeld's publication. F. Suarez, F. Poiré, J. Cartegena, H. Boudon, A. Spinelli, L. d'Argentan, J. Crasset and others[20] were all read and interesting passages noted. There is a remarkable number of texts on the spiritual maternity—quotations from the Fathers, arguments deduced from the principle of the New Eve, the Mystical Body, Scripture—

which are noted in this book, showing his intense interest in this question.[21]

Towards the close of his seminary career, Saint Louis was chosen to make the pilgrimage to Notre Dame de Chartres. His first biographer, M. Blain, has no better way to express this event than to say: "he was at the feet of his good Mother."[22] And it was at the altar of this 'good Mother' that Father Louis Mary Grignion celebrated his first Mass, at Saint Sulpice, Paris, in June 1700. Certainly the filial quality of his love for Mary still burned within his heart.

B. FROM HIS ORDINATION TO HIS DEATH (1700-1716)

The testimonies of Montfort's constant filial love for Our Lady are just as strong after his ordination, for the doctrine of the spiritual maternity was, as Alfonso Rivera declares, "the mystery of grace ... which Louis Grignion de Montfort believed himself called to preach."[23]

And Montfort did preach this truth. Not only do we know that during his missions he preached on "Mother of the Head, Mother of the Members"[24] but his biographers comment on "the tender, filial" manner with which he spoke about Our Lady.[25] This same doctrine Montfort also 'preached' in his personal letters, for there is again the constant manner of referring to Our Lady as 'my good Mother.'[26] When writing to the inhabitants of Montbernage, Poitiers, Montfort exhorts them to spread their devotion to "your good Mother" and refers to the statue of Queen of All Hearts which he had left with them as the image of 'my good Mother.'[27] His filial piety, to an extraordinary degree, has not changed.

This love for Our Lady's spiritual maternity was not restricted to his preaching and his letters but is again proved by his actions. When in open struggle with the devil he was heard to cry out from the depth of his heart: "O Blessed Virgin, my good Mother, come to my aid";[28] when in danger of being attacked by pirates while on his way to the Isle of Jersey, Montfort prayed to his good mother, then calmly told the crew: "Do not fear, Our good Mother, the Blessed Virgin, has heard our prayers."[29] The greatest proof for Montfort's constant and deep filial love for Mary is that he practiced the doctrine that he preached.

When the saint lay dying on April 28, 1716, only a few short weeks after he had been granted another vision of 'my good Mother,'[30] he must have prayed as we read in his leaflet "Preparation for a Happy Death": "give me the true heart of a son to honor her (Mary)."[31] No wonder that his intimate friend could only sum up his devotion to Mary in these words: "a confidence and a tenderness for the Blessed Virgin which has hardly any example."[32]

Throughout his entire life, therefore, the Blessed Virgin was for Saint Louis, primarily, "My Mother."

Chapter Two

The Fact of the Spiritual Maternity
in the Writings of St. Louis de Montfort

Considering the intense love of Saint Louis de Montfort for Our Lady as his good mother, we naturally expect to find this prerogative of Mary's spiritual maternity throughout his writings. And such is the case. Antonin Lhoumeau, S.M.M., does not hesitate to declare that it is found on almost every page.[33] However, before considering Montfort's explicit and implicit references to Mary's Motherhood of Men, it will be necessary to discover the place that Our Lady holds in his writings in general; only then can we see the spiritual maternity in its right perspective. We will, therefore, first take an overall, general view of all of Montfort's writings in order to discover the place of Our Lady in his system. Having put this doctrine on Our Blessed Lady in its proper setting, we can then proceed to a study of the explicit and implicit references to this privilege of the spiritual maternity.

A. THE PLACE OF OUR LADY IN THE WRITINGS OF
SAINT LOUIS DE MONTFORT

The entire doctrine of Montfort is without doubt Christocentric. Even those who are only acquainted with his *True Devotion* are well aware of this fact. So strongly does the missionary insist on the truth that Our Lord is the "Alpha and Omega, the beginning and the end of all things"[34] that he has dedicated an entire work, *The Love of the Eternal Wisdom* (probably conferences given to the seminarians of Poullart des Places) to explain the beauty and the kindness of the Second Person of the Trinity. Jesus is the final end of all his writings, for as he himself declares: "To know Jesus Christ the Eternal Wisdom is to know enough; to know everything and not to know Him, is to know nothing."[35] ". . . What will it avail us to know all other sciences necessary for salvation, if we do not know the only essential one, the science of Jesus Christ, the center to which all others must converge."[36] "Jesus Christ Our Savior, true God and true man, ought to be the last end of all our devotions, else they are false and delusive."[37] There is no doubt that the writings of Saint Louis de Montfort beautifully fulfill the words of Pope Paul VI: "In the first place it is supremely fitting that exercises of piety directed towards the Virgin Mary should clearly express the Trinitarian and Christological note that is intrinsic and essential to them."[38]

Following P. de Bérulle, J. Olier and also leaning heavily on J. St. Jure and his own contemplative study of the Wisdom literature of the Old Testament, Saint Louis de Montfort considers this final end under the aspect of Divine Wisdom: "the adorable Jesus, the Eternal and Incarnate Wisdom";[39] and to such an extent that P. Poupon can rightly remark that he has centered his entire system on this idea of Wisdom.[40] The *finis qui* or objective end of Montfort's doctrine is, therefore, Jesus Christ, the Incarnate Wisdom of the Father. Saint Louis' thought is, therefore, a Sapiential spirituality, in which we find his Marian doctrine. More than the Law and the Prophets, the Wisdom of the Father reveals the merciful kindness, the goodness and love of God; in his Incarnation, He is the humanization of God, even, as Saint Louis declares, becoming a child, poor, and dying for man upon the Cross,[41] becoming, in the Holy Spirit, intimately one with man in the depths of his being.

Saint Louis is quick to consider the subjective aspect of

this goal, the *finis quo*: union with this End, union with the Incarnate Wisdom. He is in search of a means "to acquire and conserve the Divine Wisdom."[43] The missionary would consider this union *in fieri* as a motion by which man is moved from a state of worldliness—anything keeping us back from the desired greater union with Wisdom—to an intense union with Jesus Christ, the Eternal and Incarnate Wisdom. The general theme of all Montfort's writings is concerned in some way or another with this motion of man towards union with the Eternal and Incarnate Wisdom, the ultimate goal of his 'consecration.'

In order to understand Saint Louis' explanation of this 'motion' we must recall that Saint Thomas tells us that there are three essential elements of any motion: the motion of the mover, the motion of that which is movable and the arrival at the goal.[44] Saint Louis' writings, we may say, are concerned with these three elements of our 'motion' towards union with Wisdom, all of which are found in his *Love of the Eternal Wisdom*, a true synthesis of his entire doctrine. We will consider these three elements of our movement towards Wisdom, as explained by Saint Louis.

The arrival at the goal—The terminus of this motion described by Montfort, we already know: union with Jesus, the Incarnate Wisdom. The final goal, Jesus Christ, and union with Him, are the subjects of some of the most beautiful pages he has left us.[45] Having told us of our goal, Saint Louis presents us with four means to attain Divine Wisdom,[46] the first three of which are concerned with the motion of that which is movable and the fourth, the motion of the mover.

The motion of that which is movable—The object moved is evidently man's will, and as Saint Thomas tells us, a double motion is therefore required: a motion toward the *terminus ad quem* by desire and a motion away from the *terminus a quo* by an act of detestation.[47] Saint Louis speaks of the first of these acts when he tells us that the first means to attain union with Divine Wisdom is an "ardent desire for Wisdom,"[48] a desire which is "holy and sincere, fostered by keeping the commandments."[49] This desire will express itself in prayer, which Montfort calls his second step to acquire Wisdom,[50] for prayer, as Saint Thomas declares, is *quodammodo desiderii interpres.*[51] By this persevering prayer,[52] man will beg for the greatest of all God's gifts, union with Jesus Christ, the Eternal Wisdom.[53]

In his third means, Saint Louis speaks of this withdrawal from the *terminus a quo,* when he declares that in order to leave "the spirit of the world which is contrary to Jesus Christ,"[54] we must practice universal mortification.[55] For mortification, as an *actus imperatus* of the virtue of penance, necessarily includes detestation of past wrong;[56] and if Montfort regards this mortification more as motivated by charity[57] again it necessarily includes the detestation of those things keeping us away from God.[58]

By the first three means presented by Montfort to reach union with the Eternal Wisdom—desire, prayer and mortification—the will has accomplished its withdrawal from its *terminus a quo,* the world, and its *accessus* towards its *terminus ad quem,* union with the Divine Wisdom.

The Motion of the Mover—It is when speaking about the *motio moventis* that Saint Louis develops his thought more in detail. What will bring about this desired union? Although by mortification, desire and prayer, man has fulfilled the requirements for the motion of the will, what is the motion of the mover by which man can reach his goal of union with Jesus? It is here that Montfort's doctrine on Our Lady is located. "The greatest means of all and the most wonderful of all secrets for obtaining and keeping the Divine Wisdom is a tender and true devotion to the Blessed Virgin,"[59] "for no one else has now the power to incarnate Him (the Eternal Wisdom) in the predestinate by the operation of the Holy Spirit."[60] It is Mary who "forms a man-God by grace."[61] This is then the place of Montfort's Mariology: Because of God's will, Our Lady is the hypothetically necessary means to reach union with Divine Wisdom;[62] by the grace of God she is the one who in the Holy Spirit "begets us in Jesus Christ and Jesus Christ in us."[63] The *motio moventis* is therefore, strictly speaking, sanctifying grace giving us our desired union with Divine Wisdom: but it is for Montfort a *gratia materna* as will be explained in the following pages.

Although unknown to those who are only somewhat acquainted with the doctrine of Saint Louis, his *True Devotion* and his *Secret of Mary* are but the detailed explanations of this fourth means mentioned in his *Love of the Eternal Wisdom* to attain union with Jesus Christ. It is regrettable that the place of Our Lady in Montfort's doctrine is not better known, that this 'synthesis' of his teaching is so seldom explained.[64] This lack of knowledge of Montfort's overarching Sapiential spirituality appears to be the principal reason why some authors have strongly criticized the Marian doctrine of Saint Louis de Montfort.[65]

It is evident, therefore, that for Saint Louis, Mary is principally she who will by the operation of the Spirit "incarnate Jesus in us" and who will thereby bring about this desired union with Wisdom, which is nothing less than saying that Mary is our Mother. Our Lady, therefore, enters the general plan of Saint Louis' teaching precisely as the Mother of Men—she who begets us in Jesus Christ, our Final End. Although not the prime principle of his Mariology, as we shall see, the spiritual maternity is, nonetheless, the fundamental aspect of Our Lady which he employs in his teaching.[66]

This is then the paramount place which Our Lady—and her spiritual maternity—hold in the Sapiential spirituality of Saint Louis. We will now consider the explicit and implicit references which he makes to this privilege of Mary's Motherhood of Men.

B. REFERENCES TO THE SPIRITUAL MATERNITY

Having placed the doctrine of Our Lady in its proper setting, we can now investigate the writings of Saint Louis for his references to the spiritual maternity of Our Lady. We will consider first, the implicit, and then the explicit references which Saint Louis makes to this prerogative of Our Lady.

1. *Implicit references to the Spiritual Maternity*

Saint Louis would imply that Mary is the Mother of Men when he calls Jesus, the Son of Mary, our Brother. After a 'visit' to the Christmas crib, Montfort sings in his cantiques: "Before leaving, O loving Brother, deign to bless us with your mother,"[67] or as he declares again in another Christmas hymn, "O astonishing miracle! God becomes our Brother."[68]

Moreover, the very qualities of Our Lady are those of a Mother towards her children: "She is good, she is tender, she has nothing austere and forbidding, nothing too sublime and too brilliant ... she is so charitable that she repels none of those who ask her intercession, no matter how great sinners they have been."[69] Montfort asks us to practice a devotion towards Our Lady which can only be called filial: for the qualities of a true devotion to Mary must be, according to Saint Louis, "1. interior, 2. tender, 3. holy, 4. constant and 5. disinterested."[70]

However, these implicit references are but faint shadows of Montfort's deep conviction that Mary is our Mother; this is seen when studying his explicit references to this prerogative of Our Lady.

2. *Explicit references to the Spiritual Maternity*

By no means do we intend to quote all the explicit references which Montfort makes to this privilege of Mary, for they abound in his writings. Our Lady is "Our Mother"[71] and the titles which he gives to the Mother of Men read like a special litany composed in honor of her spiritual maternity: "My good Mother,"[72] "Mother of Sweetness,"[73] "My true Mother,"[74] "Mother of the Predestinate,"[75] "The best of Mothers,"[76] "Mother of Goodness,"[77] "Mother of Gifts,"[78] "Mother of Grace,"[79] "My dear and well-beloved Mother,"[80] "His own dear Mother and Yours."[81] Echoing the Fathers, Mary is also the "Mother of the Living,"[82] "Mother of Fair Love,"[83] "Mother of Christians,"[84] "Mother of His Members."[85]

This same truth is put equivalently when Saint Louis declares: "No one but Mary has had the power to conceive and give birth to the Eternal Wisdom and no one else has now the power to incarnate Him, as it were, in the predestinate, by the operation of the Holy Spirit."[86] This basic function of Mary's Motherhood, to cooperate in our spiritual birth, is proclaimed often by Montfort: "O Blessed Virgin Mary, you give all of us life, in giving us the fruit of life";[87] "Christians, lend me your ears, listen to me, predestinate, for I tell of the marvels of her of whom you are born;"[88] "She begets them (the members of the mystical Body), bears them in her womb and brings them forth to the glory of heaven";[89] "it is my womb that has given you birth."[90]

And if Mary is Our Mother, then we are her children and Montfort is again very forceful when speaking about this term of the relationship. We are the "children of Mary,"[91] her "true children"[92] and Saint Louis, a true mystic can, therefore sing: "As a child at the breast, I am attached to her bosom, this pure and faithful Virgin nourishes me with a milk all divine."[93] Often do we find the expression: "the Blessed Virgin and her children and servants"[94] and the words which Montfort applies to himself: "the least of her children."[95] We are, therefore, according to his strong expression, "hidden in Mary's womb"[96] and can be called "the fruit of her womb."[97] Our Lady, in turn, is pictured as recognizing us as her children when Saint Louis puts these words of Saint Paul upon her lips: "I beget you every day, my dear children, until Jesus Christ my Son, be perfectly formed in you."[98]

The fact of the Spiritual Maternity is, therefore, found not only in Montfort's own spiritual life, but it abounds in his writings. We have already a glimpse of the intense love of Saint Louis for this prerogative of Our Lady; we will better understand his sublime teaching on this doctrine when we see the premises *from which he deduces this fact* of the spiritual maternity.

PART TWO

The Premises from Which Montfort Deduces
The Spiritual Maternity

Preliminary Remarks

Clearly and repeatedly does Saint Louis de Montfort proclaim the spiritual maternity of Our Blessed Mother. Not only do we find explicit expressions of this title, but it is a truth, which as we have seen, underlies his entire Marian spirituality. However, Montfort is not a mere editor, compiling a list of Mary's prerogatives; he is a theologian. As such, he cannot be content with merely stating a conclusion; he must give us the reason why he has attributed such a prerogative to the Mother of God. Theology, of which Mariology is a part, is a science and as such must proceed from certain premises by a true reasoning process.[1] What then are these premises, what is the reasoning process by which Saint Louis de Montfort arrives at the conclusion: "Mary, Our Mother?"

We must keep in mind that Saint Louis has never written a scholastic "Summa" of Mariology; however we must not think that he composed without plan or system. By no means. In examining his writings, we do see that he has a definite plan in deducing the spiritual maternity: as was not extraordinary among the writers of the French School of spirituality, the missionary begins with a study of the special relationships of Mary to the three persons of the Godhead.[2]

In doing so, he is not denying that the activity *ad extra* of the three persons is one and the same and is ascribed to one of the persons only by appropriation.[3]

However, as Karl Rahner has pointed out, this axiom deals with the efficient causality of God and does not affect the truth that the *Logos* became man or the theory of un-

created grace in which each of the three divine persons
has his own special relation to men.[4] Saint Louis would
appear to be in agreement with those theologians (e.g.
Thomassinus, Passaglia, Scheeben, Rahner) who assert
that each of the divine persons takes possession of the
justified according to their personal properties, e.g. the
Holy Spirit only takes possession of man for the Son and
for the Father, not in any hypostatic union.[5] Montfort is,
therefore, not offending orthodoxy when he brings forth
as premises from which he deduces the spiritual maternity
that such is the will of God the Father for His Daughter,
the Son for His Mother and the Holy Spirit for His
Spouse. We cannot but follow this order, the better to
convey his thought; we have therefore, arranged all of
Montfort's premises of the spiritual maternity under these
three headings, although not all are done so expressly by
him.

However, before studying these premises of the spiritual
maternity, we will first investigate the basic principle of
Montfort's Mariology. It is only by studying Saint Louis'
prime principle of Mariology that we can fully understand
the premises from which he deduces the spiritual maternity; it is only by understanding the *ratio formalis* of his
entire study on Our Lady that we can fully appreciate his
doctrine on the spiritual maternity. We will, therefore,
first consider in a preliminary chapter, the prime principle
of Saint Louis' Mariology and then study some of the
premises from which he deduces Mary's privilege of the
Spiritual Maternity.

Chapter One

The Prime Principle of
the Mariology of Saint Louis

Much has been written concerning the nature and the need of a prime principle in Mariology.[6] The question has become highly complex; we will, therefore, before searching the writings of Saint Louis for this principle, determine the nature of such a prime principle.

A. THE NATURE OF THE PRIME PRINCIPLE OF MARIOLOGY

A principle, defined by Saint Thomas as that "from which something proceeds in any manner,"[7] may be either *secundum rem* as matter and form are principles of physical bodies, or *secundum intellectum,* as premises of a conclusion. Mariology is a science—*cognitio certa per causas*—and the first principle is, therefore, evidently a principle *secundum intellectum*: that from which something is deduced and known.

We may say, therefore, that the principle of a science is that truth or proposition from which conclusions may be deduced; the conclusions will proceed from the premise by a necessity proper to that science. Theology, of which Mariology is a part, is a special science whose object is God studied under the light of revelation. Its first principle must be, therefore, a revealed truth; moreover, all conclusions must flow from this first truth, not necessarily by any metaphysical, physical or even moral necessity, but by the necessity proper to the science of theology, which is *simpliciter* in relation to those things which depend on the nature of God or are founded in the very nature of things; *hypothetical*, concerning those things which depend on the simple will of God. The privileges of Mary are evidently of this latter group.

We may, therefore, define the first principle of Mariology as that revealed truth from which all Mary's privileges may be 'scientifically' explained and from which they all flow by the hypothetical necessity of the will of God. We are, therefore, searching for the finality in God's creation of Mary. Being creative Wisdom, there is order in His plan, reason in His creation. From revealed truth, we must search for the first privilege of Mary from which it appears He has willed all other privileges to flow.

However, as is well known, certain theologians, not wishing to see the study of Our Lady as a distinct tract in theology, see no need for such a first principle;[8] others, viewing the complexity of Mariology, declare a single prime principle impossible.[9] Of the theologians who uphold a single prime principle, there are two general divisions: Mary's radical privilege is "Mother of God," or, in some way, "Prototype of the Church."[10] Within these two general divisions, there is little unanimity concerning terms used, but far more concerning the truth expressed. What is the position of Saint Louis in this question? He knew of the problem; his answer will help us put the doctrine of the spiritual maternity in its correct perspective as he sees it.

B. THE PRIME PRINCIPLE OF MARIOLOGY IN
SAINT LOUIS' WRITINGS

Nowhere in the writings of Saint Louis de Montfort can we find an explicit statement concerning his opinion on the prime principle of Mariology. Nor should this be surprising, for considering the nature of his writings, such a statement was unnecessary. Nor, as is evident, was Saint Louis acquainted with the intricacies of the problem developed by modern studies, although he was aware of the general opinion of his time concerning this prime principle.[11]

However, it is not impossible to find Saint Louis' answer to this question. A careful study of all his writings should reveal to us the radical principle from which he concludes to the other privileges of Mary. If such is found, we can presume it to be his prime principle of Mariology.

Without hesitation, we turn to the mystery of the Incarnation. Like a golden thread, the Incarnation runs throughout the writings of the holy missionary; it is "the mystery proper to the devotion"[12] he is teaching. In explaining this principal mystery of his spirituality, Saint Louis closely following de Bérulle, declares: "this mystery is an abridgement of all mysteries and contains the will and the grace of all."[13] Here we have the radical source of all mysteries, of all graces. Montfort does not consider the Incarnation speculatively, but as "the mystery of Jesus living and reigning in Mary."[14] He includes, therefore, not only the mystery of the God-Man, but also the mystery of the Divine Maternity itself. For Mary, then, the first mystery flowing from this ultimate source, the Incarnation, is her Divine Maternity. It would appear, therefore, that for Our Lady, the mystery of the Divine Maternity would be, in Montfort's eyes, the source of all her privileges and graces.

This is also insinuated by Saint Louis, so we would believe, when he tells us of the "incomparable graces that He (God) has given to Mary and particularly for having chosen her to be His Most Holy Mother."[15] In his *Cantiques,* the missionary teaches his congregation to sing: "She is the Mother of Jesus: we cannot say anything greater of her. That is the victory of victories, the crown of crowns. Let all mortals intone, in heaven, on earth and in all places: Mary is Mother of God, she is the Mother of Jesus: we cannot say anything greater of her."[16]

Moreover, it is ultimately from the Divine Maternity that Saint Louis does, de facto, deduce, not only the privilege of the Spiritual Maternity, as we shall see, but also her plenitude of grace,[17] her Immaculate Conception,[18] her Queenship,[19] her universal Mediation.[20] It does appear, therefore, that we can legitimately presume that the Divine Maternity is the source of all Mary's privileges, in the doctrine of Saint Louis.

This argument appears even stronger when we consider that it is the opinion of Father de Montfort's sources. We read in H. Boudon's *The Holy Slavery of the Admirable Mother of God*: "Her greatest happiness and which is the source of all the other favors which heaven has given her, is the Divine Maternity."[21] L. D'Argentan, in his *Grandeurs of the Blessed Virgin*, calls the Divine Maternity, "the source of all the grandeurs of the Blessed Virgin."[22] J. Crasset, in his *True Devotion to the Blessed Virgin*, declares that "the divine maternity is the foundation of all her grandeurs."[23] The thought of the French School is echoed by F. Poiré: "The first (privilege) is that of Mother of God ... where all her grandeurs ... take their origin."[24] We can, therefore, presume that such was also the opinion of Saint Louis de Montfort.

However, the missionary does not consider the Divine Maternity merely speculatively, but in its role in the history of our salvation; it is the beginning of the redemption. Saint Louis does not hesitate to sing: "God redeemed the world by the 'Hail Mary.' "[25] As we will see in greater detail when studying the premises from which Montfort deduces the spiritual maternity, there can be no doubt that the redemptive character of the Incarnation is strongly stressed in Montfort's doctrine. When we join to this fact Saint Louis' opinion that Mary is the constant "Socia Christi,"[26] it appears legitimate to conclude that Mary as Associate of the Redeemer is intrinsic, in Montfort's eyes, to the concept of Mary as the Mother of Jesus. For Saint Louis de Montfort, therefore, the source of all the privileges of Mary is the fact that she is the Mother-Associate of God the Redeemer, and such appears to be his prime principle of Mariology.[27]

Some would declare that this is the opinion of the magisterium, for Pope Paul VI in *Marialis Cultus,* when speaking about Our Lady in a general way, twice refers to her as the Mother and Associate of the Redeemer;[28] this also appears to be the tenor of the Second Vatican Council[29] and the Marian Pastoral Letter of the American Bishops.[30]

Chapter Two

The Premises of the Spiritual Maternity Based Upon the Will of the Father

"God the Father wills to have children by Mary."[31] For Saint Louis, Mary is Mother of Men because Almighty God wills that she cooperate in the bringing forth of mankind to the life of Christ. To show that such is the will of the Father, the missionary makes use of Scripture and theological arguments; he does so as a man of his time.

A. SCRIPTURE—*Ecclesiasticus* 24:13

"In Jacob inhabita: Dwell in Jacob—that is to say, make your dwelling place and residence in my children and predestined prefigured by Jacob and not in the children of the devil, the reprobate, prefigured by Esau";[32] or as it is stated in a parallel text: "It is to Mary that God the Father says: 'In Jacob inhabita: My Daughter, dwell in Jacob, that is to say, in my predestined prefigured by Jacob.'"[33] Mary is to live—to exercise her maternal functions—in the elect and the children of God.

This text has been called a 'proof' of the spiritual maternity;[34] there can be no doubt that it is only an accommodation when applied to Mary. Although Montfort does use the same text in a different sense in his *Love of the Eternal Wisdom*,[35] nonetheless, as a man of his times, he probably looked upon this text as a "scriptural proof" of Mary's Motherhood of Men. We cannot expect in Saint Louis de

27

Montfort the insights into Scripture which characterize twentieth century scholarship.

B. THEOLOGICAL ARGUMENTS

Although the basic principle in proving this will of the Father is the nature of the Mystical Body—"God the Father gave her the power to produce His Son and all the members of the Mystical Body"[36]—we will treat of this argument only when studying the will of the Son, where it is developed by Saint Louis. There are two additional arguments by which Montfort concludes to this will of the Father that Mary be the Mother of all men: the immutability of God's Will and Mary's plenitude of grace. We will consider both in detail.

1. *The Immutability of God's Will*

"The conduct which the Three Persons of the Most Holy Trinity have deigned to pursue in the Incarnation and the first coming of Jesus Christ, they still pursue daily, in an invisible manner, throughout the whole Church; and They will still pursue it even to the consummation of the ages in the last coming of Jesus Christ."[37] Therefore Montfort concludes: "God the Father wills to have children by Mary."[38] The minor which Saint Louis uses in this argumentation is his famous text: "God having willed to commence and complete His greatest works by the Holy Virgin, we may well think that He will not change His conduct, for He is God and changes not."[39] God the Father, mysteriously willing the cooperation of Mary for the Incarnation of the Word, in that very fact mysteriously wills her cooperation in the spiritual generation of men, until the end of time when the Lord will come again.

That God the Father willed to make use of Mary at the Incarnation is evident: "It was only through Mary that God the Father gave His only Begotten to the world";[40] "He gave Him (His Son) to Mary so that the world might receive Him through her."[41] Now the will of God is immutable, declares Montfort, echoing the words of Malachy 3:6: "I am the Lord and change not." Almighty God has deigned to use the cooperation of Mary at the Incarnation; therefore, in some mysterious way, her influence echoes throughout eternity.

For if Wisdom is, in Montfort's doctrine, the 'humanization' of God, even to the point of deepest intimacy with man and if this union is accomplished by a 'mystical incarnation' of the Risen Christ within us, then she who cooperates in the Incarnation of the Wisdom of the Father, also cooperates in his mystical incarnation within each one of us.

To understand the force of this argument for Montfort, we must remember that he considers our sanctification, our spiritual generation to have already taken place in principle at the Incarnation. As we shall see, not only does he declare that at the Incarnation we are redeemed[42] but all the elect have been chosen in this mystery.[43] Our particular generation at baptism is then for Montfort, but the 'application in time' of what was already effected in principle at the Incarnation. Montfort sees no reason why he cannot, therefore, conclude to our spiritual generation by Mary from the will of God shown in the Incarnation. It does appear valid to conclude with Saint Louis that since God freely required the cooperation of Mary at the redemptive Incarnation, this will of the Father and the cooperation of Mary perdure as redemption is carried out, or as it is sometimes put, if Mary cooperates *in actu primo*, then it follows that she cooperates *in actu secundo*. For Montfort, *redemption is one*, and her cooperation at the Incarnation proves that in some mysterious way she is cooperating now in the redemption of mankind and her cooperation will not be completed until that day when Jesus, the Eternal and Incarnate Wisdom, is 'incarnated' spiritually in mankind.

As the Bishops of the United States declared in their

Marian Pastoral: "What Mary began on earth in association with the saving mission of Jesus, she continues still
in union with the risen Christ."[44] It is interesting to note
that one of the points of agreement between Catholic and
non-Catholic theologians at the International Mariological
Marian Congress in Rome, 1975, was: "6. Prayers of
intercession directed to the Blessed Virgin Mary have
as the foundation, besides the confidence which the Holy
Spirit has raised up among the Christian people towards
the Mother of God, also the fact that Mary remains always
connected to the work of Redemption and therefore to its
application throughout times and places."[45]

2. Mary's Plenitude of Grace

The Will of God the Father is made evident not only
by the preceding argument but also by the plenitude of
grace which He was pleased to grant Mary.[46] The question of employing this privilege of Mary as a premise from
which we deduce the spiritual maternity has been the subject of important study, especially by the Spanish School
of Mariology.[47] Montfort's argument may thus be formu-
lated: Our Lady's fullness of grace has been divinely constituted to overflow upon men. Now it is by grace that
we are spiritually born; therefore, Mary has been divinely
constituted to give us birth. This argument is found
repeatedly in the writings of Saint Louis.

However, before examining Saint Louis' development of
the problem, we must note that he appears to distinguish
two types of plenitude in Mary: what we may term a
plenitudo canalis and a *plenitudo fontis*.[48] Considering
Our Lady as possessing the plenitude of a canal, Montfort
at times declares that she has been constituted the dis-
tributor of the plenitude of Christ; it is not of her own
plenitude that we receive, but the fullness of Our Lord.
By what we may call *plenitudo fontis*, however, Montfort
seems at times to say that she gives us of her own fullness, of her own overflowing plenitude. We will, therefore,

consider Mary's plenitude in both senses given us by Montfort, and then consider their respective value as arguments for the spiritual maternity.

a) Mary's *Plenitudo canalis*—Our Lady has been divinely appointed to play a mysterious role in the total plan of redemption. It is through her cooperation as Mother-Associate of God the Redeemer that we share in the divine life; therefore Mary has been divinely appointed our Mother. This *plenitudo canalis* is clearly expressed in the writings of Saint Louis which, in the figurative language of the times makes grace appear to be a corporeal entity: "God the Son communicated to His Mother all that He acquired by His life and His death, His infinite merits and His admirable virtues; and He has made her the treasurer of all that His Father gave Him for His inheritance. It is by her that He applies His merits to His members and that He communicates His virtues and distributes His graces. She is His mysterious canal; she is His aqueduct, through which He makes His mercies flow gently and abundantly."[49]

This privilege of Mary is also brought out by Saint Louis when comparing her role as Mother of men to that of Rebecca: "This good Mother clothes us in the clean, new, precious and perfumed garments of Esau the elder —that is of Jesus Christ her Son—which she keeps in her house, that is, which she has in her own power, inasmuch as she is the treasurer and universal dispenser of the merits and virtues of her Son, which she gives and communicates to whom she wills, when she wills, as she wills and in such quantity as she wills."[50]

In his book on the Eternal Wisdom, Saint Louis again states this opinion: "She is ... the immense ocean of all the grandeurs of God, the great storehouse of all his goods, the inexhaustible treasure of the Lord and the Treasurer and Dispenser of all His gifts ... He gives no celestial gift to this earth without having it pass by her as by a canal ... It is of her fullness that we have all received. ..."[51] And as Saint Louis de Montfort tells us, it is by grace that we are born;[52] Mary is therefore constituted our Mother.

b) Mary's *Plenitudo Fontis*—Montfort also seems to attribute to Mary a *plenitudo fontis,* declaring that it is Mary's own grace which overflows upon men.

In his *Secret of Mary,* Saint Louis boldly states: "Whoever wishes to be a member of Jesus Christ, must be formed in Mary by the grace of Jesus Christ which resides in her in its plenitude, to be communicated to the true members of Jesus Christ and to his true children."[53] It is a grace 'residing' in Mary; but it is the grace of Jesus Christ, and therefore, probably should be classified as a *plenitudo canalis.* But the missionary expresses his thoughts in clearer terms: "She gives her whole self, and gives it in an unspeakable manner, to him who gives all to her. She causes him to be engulfed in the abyss of her graces. She adorns him with her merits."[54] Explaining his third interior practice of Holy Slavery, "All in Mary," Montfort declares "in that virginal womb, the soul shall be nourished with the milk of her grace and maternal mercy";[55] according to the example used, it appears to be Mary's life, the overflowing of her plenitude. We are told in the *Cantiques* that Mary was filled with grace at Pentecost, even for us,[56] that she was filled with Wisdom, even for us.[57]

Stronger still does this opinion become when we consider these words of the *True Devotion* which follow Montfort's statement that Mary is the canal of the merits and virtues of Jesus Christ: "She bestows a new perfume and a new grace on their garments and adornments in communicating to them (her children) her own garments, that is, her merits and virtues, which she bequeathed to them by her testament when she died ... thus all her domestics and faithful servants and slaves are doubly clad in the garments of Jesus and in her own."[58]

Pope Paul uses somewhat the same language when he declares: "These virtues of the Mother will also adorn her children who steadfastly study her example in order to reflect it in their own lives."[59]

c) *Value of these Arguments.* Before considering the value of these arguments in proving the spiritual maternity, it is necessary to learn exactly what Montfort implies when telling us that Mary gives us of the plenitude of Christ and also of her own plenitude.

Stripped of their poetical expressions, both statements do imply that Our Lady has been divinely appointed as some type of principle in the "distribution of grace." However, when declaring that it is of Mary's own plenitude that we receive, Saint Louis would seem to imply that Mary has, in some way, with Christ and subordinately to Him merited these graces for us and they can be called, therefore, her graces, her virtues.

If we pierce through the imagery and the poetical language of the era of Louis XIV, it appears that Montfort is telling us in all these texts (both those considered as referring to *plenitudo canalis* and *plenitudo fontis*), that Mary has played a mysterious and efficacious role in the redemptive Incarnation; the gift of God's Love has been united to her *fiat.* Therefore the redemption itself bears the imprint of her mysterious cooperation which continues for all eternity. To come closer to Montfort's language, we can call all grace, *gratia materna* because of this association of Mary in the redemption of the universe through her cooperation—willed by the Father—in the redemptive Incarnation.

Because of this cooperation, we can speak of Mary as possessing the *plenitudo canalis* and the *plenitudo fontis.* The *plenitudo fontis stresses* Mary's role in the redemption of men; the precise nature of this role will be seen when discussing the theological arguments Montfort employs in deducing the spiritual maternity from the will of the Son.

This argument is, therefore, similar to that employed by Montfort when speaking of the immutability of God's Will: Mary plays an efficacious role in the redemption of mankind through her consent at the Incarnation. Validly, therefore, does Montfort conclude to her spiritual maternity. It is beautiful to see how Montfort, the missionary, takes this central argument and explains it to his simple people in their terms, in their language so that they can truly understand the reality of Mary's spiritual maternity.

Having completed his 'proofs' that God the Father wills that Mary be the Mother of men, Saint Louis de Montfort rightfully concludes: "As in the natural and corporal generation there is a father and a mother, likewise in the supernatural and spiritual generation, there is a father who is God and a mother who is Mary"[60] or as it is stated in a parallel text: "As in the natural order, it is necessary that a true child of the Church have God for His Father and Mary for His Mother."[61] It is a legitimate comparison of a missionary to impress upon his listeners the truth of Mary's spiritual maternity.[62] In order to make this prerogative of Our Lady even more evident and in order to show that this privilege of Mary is a result of the will of the Father, Saint Louis repeats the comparison from the negative view: "Who does not have Mary for Mother, has not God for Father ... Alas, God the Father has not told Mary to make her dwelling place in them, for they are Esaus."[63]

Chapter Three

The Premises of the Spiritual Maternity Based Upon the Will of the Holy Spirit

"God the Holy Spirit wills to form elect for Himself in her (Mary) and by her."[64] Mary is the Mother of men, for it is, according to Saint Louis de Montfort, the gracious will of the Holy Spirit that she cooperate with Him in the spiritual generation of men, by which He takes possession of man for the Father through the Son.

As he did to demonstrate the will of the Father, so too, the missionary now employs both Scripture and theological arguments to show that the Holy Spirit wills Mary's cooperation in His work of sanctification.

A. SCRIPTURE—*Ecclesiasticus* 24:13

Montfort again uses Ecclesiasticus 24:13 to explicitate his assertion that God the Holy Spirit wills to have children by Mary. The missionary applies the third part of this verse to the Will of the Holy Spirit: *"In electis meis mitte radices.* Take root, my Beloved and my Spouse, of all your virtues in my elect."[65] In the parallel text in the *Secret of Mary,* Saint Louis declares: "It is to Mary that the Holy Spirit has said: *In electis meis mitte radices*: Take root, my faithful spouse, in my elect."[66] Mary is, therefore, to 'produce' her virtues in the souls of men. The similarity here with Mary as the *plenitudo canalis et fontis* is evident.

There can be no doubt that this is an accommodation of

35

the Scriptural text. As mentioned above, considering the use of the 'senses' of Scripture at the time of Montfort, it may well be that he saw in this text some type of true Scriptural foundation for the spiritual maternity.

B. THEOLOGICAL ARGUMENTS

"Take root, My Beloved and My Spouse, of all your virtues in my elect."[67] Saint Louis here announces his two theological principles which he develops in order to demonstrate that it is the gracious will of the Holy Spirit that Mary be the Mother of men: she is the Well-Beloved of the Holy Spirit and she is His Spouse. After considering Montfort's insights into these two prerogatives of Mary, we will examine their validity as premises of the spiritual maternity and also consider the fittingness of his arguments in this post Vatican II age.

1. *The Well-Beloved of the Holy Spirit*

Because of the complacence of the Holy Spirit in Mary's great virtues, He wishes these same virtues reproduced by Mary in men; she must in the power of the Spirit, 'generate' in us the virtues which she possesses in their fulness. Several times in his writings, Montfort employs this reasoning.

The missionary explains to his congregation, first of all, the "sublime virtues" of Our Lady. "She is," he boldly declares, "the magnificence of the Most High."[68] "The height of her merits ... cannot be fully seen ... the breadth of her charity ... is in truth immeasurable ... the depth of her humility and of all her virtues and graces is an abyss which can never be sounded. O height incomprehensible, O breadth unspeakable, O length immeasurable, O abyss impenetrable!"[69] So great are the virtues of Our Lady that the knowledge and possession of her, God has reserved for Himself.[70]

Saint Louis pictures the Holy Spirit taking complacence

in the unspeakable virtues of His Spouse and has Him say:
"I took so much complacence in you when you lived on
earth in the practice of the most sublime virtues."[71] Because God the Holy Spirit is 'well-pleased' with the virtues
of Our Lady, He says to her: "I desire to find you still
on earth without your ceasing to be in heaven"[72] and to
accomplish this desire, Mary is told: "Reproduce your-
self in my elect ... that I may behold in them with complacence the roots of your invincible faith, of your profound humility, of your universal mortification, of your
sublime prayer, of your ardent charity, of your firm hope
and of all your virtues."[73]

So great, therefore, is the complacence of the Holy Spirit in the virtues of Mary, which He Himself has produced,
that He wishes that these be found in the members of the
Mystical Body. Mary must, therefore, "communicate her
own garments, that is, her merits and virtues"[74] so that
we may become "living copies of Mary"[75] and the Holy
Spirit can then find "His dear Spouse reproduced, as it
were, in souls."[76] In summary, we can say that it is the
will of the Holy Spirit that Mary 'give birth' to these virtues in men, for the Holy Spirit desires to see His Spouse,
His Masterpiece, 'duplicated' in men. The value of these
expressions, couched in the language of a fiery missionary,
must be examined to discover their worth; we will do so
after completing his second and principal argumentation
from the will of the Holy Spirit: Mary is the Spouse of
the Holy Spirit, Whose task is the sanctification of men.

2. *The Spouse of the Holy Spirit*

Mary is the Mother of men, not so much, according to
Montfort, because of the complacence of the Holy Spirit
in her virtues, but because she is the Spouse of the Holy
Spirit. "The Holy Spirit, having espoused Mary ... continues to produce continually in her and by her, in a mysterious and true manner, the predestinate."[77]

By employing the analogy of 'spouse,' Saint Louis evi-

dently wants to portray Our Lady not only as a companion of the Holy Spirit but in a union with Him, which,
like any true marriage is considered indissoluble and ordi-
narily fruitful. Montfort insists upon these three elements or rather this union with its two qualities of indissolubility and fruitfulness, when proclaiming Our Lady
the Spouse of the Holy Spirit. From his contemplative
theologizing on the ramifications of this title—and
strongly influenced by de Bérulle and Olier—he deduces
the spiritual maternity. He sees in this role of Mary as
'Spouse of the Spirit' the fact that Our Lady has been
united indissolubly to the Third Person of the Trinity, in
the work of the sanctification of men, which will only be
complete when all creation will be one in Christ Jesus;
even then, in that glory which eye has not seen nor ear
heard, Mary remains associated in a unique way with the
dynamic workings of the Spirit. We will, therefore, examine the three qualities which for Montfort are included
in the term 'Spouse' and which necessarily must be included, if it is to be a principle for the spiritual maternity
in the entire work of redemption.

a. The Union of Mary and the Holy Spirit

By the use of the term 'spouse,' we are made aware of
a certain union between Mary and God the Holy Spirit,
for the definition of spouse connotes this. When Saint
Louis repeatedly calls Mary "Spouse of the Holy Spirit,"[78]
he implies, therefore, this intimate spiritual union between
Mary and the Second Person of the Trinity.[79]

With what right does Saint Louis proclaim this espousal? Again, faithful to the French school of spirituality,
he has recourse to his 'principal mystery,' the Incarnation.

Although filled with the graces of the Holy Spirit from
the time of her Immaculate Conception,[80] it is especially
at the annunciation that she enters into a mysterious union
with Him: "God the Holy Spirit...has become fruitful
by Mary whom He has espoused. It was with her, in her

and of her that He produced His Masterpiece which is a
God made man."[81] "The Substantial Love of the Father
and the Son has espoused Mary, in order to produce Jesus
Christ."[82] Since by her *fiat* Mary becomes, by the overshadowing of the Holy Spirit, the means by which Wisdom
came into our human race, and bolstered by his firm belief
that the title "spouse of the Spirit" is patristic and the
common teaching of the Church, Saint Louis concludes to
the legitimacy of this title and the indissoluble union it
implies.

Montfort is, however, careful to avoid the danger which
Saint Thomas calls to mind of deducing that the Holy
Spirit is, therefore, the father of Jesus,[83] when he writes:
"What a great mystery! the shadow alone of the Holy
Spirit formed in her Jesus Christ, made her His Mother,
without becoming the father."[84] Saint Louis, insisting so
strongly on Mary as Spouse of the Holy Spirit, under-
standably also stresses the special intimate union which
exists between Our Lady and the Third Person of the
Blessed Trinity.

b. The Indissolubility of this Union

The Holy Spirit called forth the free cooperation of
Mary in the Incarnation of the Wisdom of the Father and
therefore Our Lady can be called His Spouse. However,
in order to deduce from this title the spiritual maternity,
Saint Louis also declares that this union is indissoluble;
it exists not only for the Incarnation of the Divine Wisdom
but also for all times, for the spiritual generation of all
men.

Mary is the Spirit's "faithful and indissoluble Spouse.
I say: faithful and indissoluble Spouse. . .";[85] she is "the
indissoluble companion (words which Montfort also uses
for the Son) of the Holy Spirit for all works of grace"
and this because of "a singular grace (which she has received) from the Most High."[86] "He (the Holy Spirit) has
never repudiated her because she has always been fruitful

and faithful."[87] To demonstrate this indissolubility, Saint
Louis also makes use of some arguments explained above,
i.e., the unity of the Divine plan of redemption and the
immutability of God's Will. For if the sanctification of
men is seen as already having taken place in principle at
the Incarnation of the Divine Wisdom, the missionary
readily concludes that since Mary was chosen to cooperate
in the Incarnation, she is always the Spouse of the Spirit,
even now in the mystical incarnation of Divine Wisdom
in the souls of men. There is no doubt in Montfort's mind
that this espousal of the Holy Spirit and Mary is for all
times, is continual, embracing not only the Incarnation
of the Word of God but the spiritual generation of mankind.

c. The fruitfulness of This Union

A union which is indissoluble is not enough to prove
that Mary is truly the Mother of men. We know that this
union—this overshadowing of the Holy Spirit—was fruitful in the begetting of the God-Man; Montfort also as-
serts that this union is actually fruitful in the spiritual
life of men.

Saint Louis implicitly proves that this union is fruitful
in the sanctification of men, for he tells us that the Holy
Spirit's work is the sanctification of mankind, the spiritual generation of men: "It is you alone who form all the
divine persons outside of the Divinity";[88] "Come, Holy
Spirit, who form the martyrs, the confessors, the apostles,
the prophets, the great heroes, the great hearts."[89] The
Holy Spirit is then, THE principle of our sanctification.
In no way can it be said that in Montfort's doctrine Mary
supplants or takes the place of the Holy Spirit in man's
sanctification. Mary, through the goodness of the Most
High and only because of the will of God, is the "insepar-
able companion of the Holy Spirit in all works of grace."[90]
She is, as we have seen, in an indissoluble union with her
Spouse, the principle of our spiritual generation. She must,

therefore, in Montfort's eyes, cooperate, subordinately and dependently as he insists, in the actual generation of men spiritually; she shares, in this sense, in his fruitfulness.

However, Montfort elucidates this point when he declares: "You (the Holy Spirit) have formed the Head of the predestinate with her and in her; it is with her and in her that You must form all His members";[91] "having produced in her and of her Jesus Christ, this Masterpiece, the Incarnate Word ... He continues to produce daily in her and by her ... the predestinate";[92] and as he declares in his *True Devotion*, the Holy Spirit produces with her and in her Jesus Christ and His members.[93]

We come again, in discussing the fruitfulness of Mary through and in the Holy Spirit, to the core of the mystery of the spiritual maternity in the doctrine of Saint Louis de Montfort: the mystery of the union of Head and members of the Body of Christ. In actual fact, the missionary is repeating this one proof over and over again, considering different facets of the same argument: Mary is chosen by the grace of God to cooperate in a unique way in our redemption at the Incarnation; therefore, in some mysterious way, considering the nature of the redemptive incarnation, her cooperation continues until the Lord comes again and we shall be one in the Lord Jesus Christ, in the power of the Spirit, to the praise of the Father. Mary is, therefore, the Mother of men.

However, numbers 20, 21, of the *True Devotion*, concerning the 'fruitfulness of Mary' have been the subject of controversy since the discovery of the manuscript in 1842. Pusey, Newman and Faber were embroiled in it[94] as were theologians of the 1940's and 1950's[95] and even quite recently these lines of the *True Devotion* were discussed in talks delivered at the annual meetings of the *Société Française d'Etudes Mariales*.[96]

Because of the importance given to these two numbers, it is best that they be quoted in full: "God the Holy Spirit, being barren in God, that is to say, not producing another

Divine Person, is become fruitful by Mary, whom He has espoused. It was with her, in her and of her that He produced His Masterpiece, which is God made Man and that He goes on producing daily, to the end of the world, the predestinate and the members of the Body of that adorable Head. This is the reason why He, the Holy Spirit, the more He finds Mary, His dear and inseparable Spouse, in any soul, the more active and mighty He becomes in producing Jesus Christ in that soul and that soul in Jesus Christ. It is not that we mean that Our Blessed Lady gives the Holy Spirit His fruitfulness, as if He had it not Himself. For inasmuch as He is God, He has the same fruitfulness or capacity of producing as the Father and the Son; only He does not bring it into act, as He does not produce another Divine Person. But what we mean is, that the Holy Spirit chose to make use of Our Blessed Lady, though He had no absolute need of her, to bring His fruitfulness into act, by producing in her and by her Jesus Christ and His members, a mystery of grace unknown to even the wisest and most spiritual of Christians."[97]

The text surely insists upon the fruitfulness of Mary in the sanctification of men. Mary is, for Montfort, the Well-Beloved of the Spirit, and even more important, His Spouse, united to Him in an indissoluble, fruitful union. What is the value of these teachings of the missionary as 'proofs' for the spiritual maternity? What is the fittingness of the terms used, the 'orthodoxy' of these statements?

3. *The Value of these Arguments*

We have seen, first of all, that Montfort insists upon the complacence of the Holy Spirit in the virtues of Mary and, therefore, wishes to see these reproduced in men. Are these adequate premises for the deduction of the spiritual maternity of Mary?

What does this complacence prove? Besides repeating

in a different form his argument based upon the *plenitudo fontis,* it appears that Saint Louis is stating in the oratorical language of his day what is insisted upon in the Second Vatican Council: Mary is, subordinately and dependently on Christ, the pattern, the model of all Christians.[98] Understood in this sense, it is not a theological proof of the spiritual maternity, for it does not in itself lead to the conclusion that Mary has the *power* to reproduce these virtues in man as their spiritual mother. Rather, the argument when taken alone is a statement of fact, depending upon the entire context to supply the adequate theological reasoning for this prerogative. It is, therefore, no additional argument for the spiritual maternity, but presupposes Montfort's principal 'proof' based upon the nature of the Mystical Body (to be seen later) which, in fact, immediately precedes, in the *True Devotion,* this explanation of the complacence of the Holy Spirit in the excellence of Mary's God-given virtues.

A critique of Saint Louis' arguments based upon Our Lady, Spouse of the Holy Spirit, is more difficult; to unravel the intricate theological knots woven by years of argumentation, often with a disregard for the rules of hermeneutics and with strong partisan tendencies, is almost impossible. Nonetheless, we will attempt to clarify Montfort's position, considering first the legitimacy and fittingness of the title "Spouse of the Holy Spirit"; secondly, its value—as used by Montfort—as a proof of the spiritual maternity and finally, we must consider the orthodoxy of his argumentation, so often challenged.

It must be stated categorically that the non-Scriptural title "Spouse of the Holy Spirit" is, in spite of Saint Louis de Montfort's opinion, not to be considered a common teaching of the Fathers of the Church. Montfort is leaning heavily on his sources, especially de Bérulle, Olier, Poiré, when he writes in his *Notebook*: "She is the Spouse of the Holy Spirit—a great number of the Fathers of the Church give us testimony of it."[99] The source of this notation is

F. Poiré, who in his *Triple Crown* declares that it is even useless "to go to the trouble of proving this truth, since all the Fathers unanimously (*sic!*) preached it and it is the ordinary teaching of the Catholic Church."[100]

Poiré has undoubtedly exaggerated, and Montfort uncritically accepted his position. J. Terrien declares more soberly: "It is necessary to admit that, as frequent as the appellation of Spouse of the Holy Spirit attributed to the Blessed Virgin may be today, it was practically unknown to the early writers"[101] and he declares to have scarcely found the expression twice in his search through the early literature of the Church. It would appear, then, that Poiré bases his assertions on implicit citations of this title, e.g. *sacrarium Spiritus Sancti* which, as Poupon remarks, when applied to a living person is equivalently declaring such a person a mystic spouse.[102] However, the title does become common in the Middle Ages and has often been employed, even by the magisterium (e.g. Leo XIII in *Divinum illud munus;* Pius XII in his *Radiomessage for the crowning of Our Lady of Fatima*) to express the intimate union between Mary and the Holy Spirit.

However, the Second Vatican Council, implicitly underlining the fact that between the Spirit and a creature there cannot exist that reciprocity which characterizes conjugal union, purposefully avoids the title; in its place we find 'sacrarium,' 'sanctuary,' 'temple.' Paul VI, in *Marialis Cultus,* although devoting a special section to Mary and the Holy Spirit, follows the Vatican Council and never calls Our Lady the Spouse of the Holy Spirit, although he does declare: "they (some Fathers and writers of the Church) saw in the mysterious relationship between the Spirit and Mary an aspect redolent of marriage, poetically portrayed by Prudentius: 'The unwed Virgin espoused the Spirit'..."[103]

Montfort appears to use the title in an orthodox manner, for it connotes for him Mary's intimate union with the Spirit, through her consent to the redemptive Incarnation, in His task of uniting us to the Father through Christ. Although the title may have been a fitting one in the context of Montfort's preaching, in today's biblical and ecumenical atmosphere, this title, easily given to misunderstanding, would be best avoided.

Considering the meaning which the contemplative preacher intended to convey by 'Spouse of the Holy Spirit,' he can, as we have seen, conclude to the spiritual maternity. For he is, through the ramifications of this title, paraphrasing his principal argument that Mary has, through her efficacious consent to the Incarnation, uniquely cooperated in the Spirit's work of sanctification and, therefore, is rightly called Our Mother.

We can question the fittingness of the term 'Spouse of the Holy Spirit,' although admitting that it is, for Montfort, a valid proof of Mary's spiritual maternity. Can we declare unorthodox Montfort's words in numbers 20, 21 of the *True Devotion* when he speaks of the fruitfulness of this espousal?

In attempting to answer this delicate, complex question, we should keep in mind that especially when proclaiming a mystery of the faith, no preacher can ever succeed in fully saying what he means, because his thoughts have to be expressed in such limited objective structures in which, as Schillebeeckx well declares, his ideas are, so to speak, dispossessed.[104] Moreover, in trying to judge Montfort's meaning, we have to recall that an intricate maze of presuppositions, many unknown in any conscious manner by the missionary himself, play an important role. Nonetheless, to the best of our ability, we must probe into this question of the orthodoxy of Saint Louis' argumentation, for it has been the subject of so many discussions.

In speaking of Mary's relationship with the Holy Spirit, Montfort seems to be desperately caught up in the impossibility of expressing his contemplative insights within objective structures. Leaning on his predecessors, especially d'Argentan, and almost quoting de Bérulle,[105]

Montfort, the preacher, the mystic, declares that the Holy Spirit, "being barren in God, not producing another Divine Person, is become fruitful by Mary whom He has espoused."[106] Now if Saint Louis stopped here, as G. Philips implies de Bérulle does,[107] we could declare that this is, for our own day, a rather striking if not unfortunate way of expressing traditional Trinitarian theology that the Father generates the Son and that the Father and the Son spirate the Holy Spirit, while the Spirit neither generates nor spirates. Speaking of the Spirit's sterility *ad intra*, and his fecundity *ad extra*, can evidently lead to serious misunderstandings. However, as G. Philips points out, Saint Louis "felt the weakness and the danger (of de Bérulle's stance) for he adds a restrictive commentary which brings him back to the reality of the current affirmations of theology."[108]

Saint Louis does this not only through the immediate context (especially numbers 17-19 of the *True Devotion*) and by his overall thought gleaned from a study of all his writings, but by immediately adding to the statement taken from de Bérulle, a warning: "It is not that we mean that Our Blessed Lady gives the Holy Spirit His fruitfulness, as if He had it not Himself. For inasmuch as He is God, He has the same fruitfulness or capacity of producing as the Father and the Son; only He does not bring it into act, as He does not produce another Divine Person. But what we mean is, that the Holy Spirit chose to make use of Our Blessed Lady, though He had no absolute need of her, to bring His fruitfulness into act by producing in her and by her Jesus Christ and His members."[109]

G. Philips declares that this is excellently stated, comparable to Saint Augustine.[110] Nonetheless, if Montfort had limited himself to declaring along with de Bérulle that there is in the Holy Spirit an *ad intra* sterility which becomes an *ad extra* fecundity in Mary, we could speak of its almost unintelligibility to us today. Some would wish that Montfort had omitted this complicated and easily misunderstood expression of the French School of spirituality; however, he is a man of his time, and it is to his credit that he did add the corrective explanations mentioned above.

In summary, we can say that Montfort appears almost tongue-tied, confused, in face of this great mystery of Mary's union with the Holy Spirit; his "it is not that we mean" ... "but what we mean" betray this felt impossibility of saying what he means, since his contemplative thoughts have to be expressed in the 'alienation' of language. His respect for his sources seems to force him to try to explain the mystery through their words (no. 20) which he apparently realizes can be misleading and he therefore offers an explanation (no. 21). We cannot judge his opinion concerning the Spirit's role and Mary's fruitfulness solely from these two complex numbers of the *True Devotion* but from his overall doctrine which we have attempted to outline above. The problem of these few sentences of the *True Devotion* should not be exaggerated.

Because Our Lady is the Well-Beloved of the Spirit, because she is His Spouse, Montfort concludes that it is the will of the Third Person of the Trinity that Mary be the Mother of men. This teaching is resuméd in his *Prayer to Jesus*: "O Holy Spirit, give me a great devotion ... to Mary, Thy divine Spouse,[111] a great confidence in her maternal bosom, a continual recourse to her mercy, so that in her you may form in me Jesus Christ, to His likeness, great and mighty, unto the fulness of His perfect age. Amen."[112]

Chapter Four

The Premises of the Spiritual Maternity
Based Upon the Will of the Son

"God the Son wishes to form Himself, and so to speak, incarnate Himself in His members by His dear Mother."[113] With these strong terms, Saint Louis proclaims that the Second Person of the Blessed Trinity, the Eternal and Incarnate Wisdom, desires that Mary be the Mother of all men, that she cooperate in His spiritual incarnation in the hearts of men.

Since, according to Montfort, the very purpose of the spiritual maternity is to 'incarnate' Jesus in us by grace, he speaks of Mary's relation to the Incarnate Wisdom in some detail, in order to come to the conclusion that Mary is our Mother. On this point, arguments from Scripture, Tradition, and theological reasoning can be found interspersed throughout his writings.

A. Arguments from Scripture

Five texts are employed by Montfort: Genesis 3:15; Ecclesiasticus 24:13; Psalm 87:5 Luke 1:26-38 and John 19:26-27.

1. *Genesis 3:15.* The text of the protoevangelium is well known: "I will place enmities between thee and the woman, between thy seed and her seed. She shall crush thy head and thou shalt lie in wait for her heel." This is the translation which Montfort used and it is upon this

translation that he bases his arguments. Modern scholarship has given us a more faithful translation: "I will put enmity between you and the woman and between your seed and her seed; he shall bruise your head and you shall bruise his heel" (Revised Standard Version).

Since the time of Saint Justin, this verse and its Marian interpretations have been the subject of divergent opinions. Montfort's interpretation of this text is relatively easy to ascertain, for he treats of it explicitly in numbers 51-54 of his *True Devotion*. There can be no doubt, that Saint Louis, as a man of his age, sees Our Lady—in apparently a strict Scriptural sense—as the "Woman" of the Protoevangelium. After quoting the biblical text, the missionary comments: "God has made and formed but one enmity; but it is an irreconcilable one which shall endure and grow to the end. It is between Mary . . . and the devil—between the children and the servants of the Blessed Virgin and the children and the tools of Lucifer. The most terrible of all the enemies which God has set up against the devil is His Holy Mother. He has inspired her, even since the days of the earthly paradise, though she existed then only in His idea, with so much hatred against that cursed enemy of God . . ."[114]

Montfort, moreover, sees in this text the spiritual maternity of Our Lady, for the 'seed of the Woman' comprises all the children of Mary. The enmity is, therefore, between the "children of the Blessed Virgin and the children of Lucifer."[115] "God has set not only an enmity but enmities, antipathies and secret hatreds, between the true children and servants of Mary and the children and slaves of the devil."[116] Speaking figuratively, Saint Louis calls these children of Mary, Our Lady's heel, for "they shall be little and poor in the world's esteem and abased before all, like the heel."[117] But, continues Montfort, "they shall, in union with Mary, crush the head of the devil."[118]

There can be no doubt, therefore, that Montfort sees the spiritual maternity as divinely revealed in Genesis

3:15, although never using it explicitly as a proof for this prerogative.

It should be noted that leading scholars in Old Testament studies, such as Skinner,[119] not only do not see any Marian interpretation possible but even declare that the text in itself does not point to any victory or hope for salvation. Although before the Second Vatican Council, many Catholic scholars saw in the protoevangelium a reference to Mary in a strict literal sense,[120] today more are inclined to agree with Charles Miller's conclusion: "It seems clear that Vatican II's Mariological reference to Gn 3:15 in LG (*Lumen Gentium*) is really more an appeal to Tradition than to a proof-text from the Old Testament. Literally, the text says nothing about the woman sharing in the victory of her seed over the serpent, if indeed there be such a victory. Even the patristic tradition itself, furthermore, is not unanimous on the Mariological significance of the passage. At most, it might be considered as an example of *sensus plenior*."[121]

It must be recalled that when this text is used in the Second Vatican Council's *Constitution on the Church* it is qualified by the statement: "The books of the Old Testament recount the period of salvation history during which the coming of Christ into the world was slowly prepared for. These earliest documents as they are read in the Church and are understood in the light of a further and full revelation, bring the figure of the Woman, Mother of the Redeemer, into a gradually sharper focus. When looked at in this way, she is already prophetically foreshadowed in that victory over the serpent which was promised to our first parents after their fall into sin (cf. Gn 3:15)."[122]

It would not appear, therefore, that the protoevangelium can be used as a *strict Scriptural proof* in Mariology; it is, however, through this text that the Church has expressed its teaching on Mary's role in salvation history and it can be used as a proof from the tradition of the Church.

It is probably in this sense that Pope Paul declares in *Marialis Cultus,* no. 30: "the Bible is replete with the mystery of the Savior, and from Genesis to the Book of Revelation also contains clear references to her who was the Mother and Associate of the Savior." The same thought is expressed by the American Bishops in their Marian Pastoral, *Behold Your Mother,* no. 19: "The light of completion shows that the Redeemer's Mother was 'already prophetically foreshadowed in that victory over the serpent which was promised to our first parents....'"

Although few theologians today would therefore accept Saint Louis' exegesis of this text, it must always be remembered that we cannot take the missionary out of the thought patterns of his own time. In the beginning of the 18th century, Montfort's interpretation of Genesis 3:15 would have been accepted not only by the common people, but by scholars also. His commentary on Genesis 3:15 does show us his firm belief in the spiritual maternity of Our Lady, and his conviction that this prerogative is found in the inspired Word of God.

2. *Ecclesiasticus 24:13.* "In Israel haereditare ... Have Israel for your inheritance"[123] or as it is said in a parallel text: "It is to Mary that God the Son has said: 'In Israel haereditare': My dear Mother, have your heritage in Israel, that is to say, in the predestined."[124]

Basing himself again on the fact that Israel is a figure of the predestined and Esau of the reprobate, Saint Louis, unlike all scholars today, employs this text probably as a proof of the spiritual maternity, in accordance with the principles of Scriptural interpretation of his sources. As Montfort himself explains the text, it would signify that Our Lady has the predestined for her possession and therefore the Lord says to her: "as their good mother you will give them birth, nourish them and raise them and, as their queen, you will conduct, govern and defend them."[125]

3. *Psalm 87:5.* "A man and a man are born in her, says the Holy Spirit, *Homo et homo natus est in ea.* According

to the explanation of some of the Fathers, the first man who is born of Mary is the Man-God, Jesus Christ; the second is a mere man, child of God and of Mary by adoption."[126] Montfort, basing himself on the translation of this psalm used in his day and upon the interpretation of the Fathers (which he received second-hand from the writers he knew) implies that this text applies to the spiritual maternity. There is no doubt that the Marian interpretation is an accommodation; Montfort knew of the Marian use of this text through the Liturgy and also through the Marian interpretations of some of his favorite spiritual authors, especially Olier.[127]

Saint Louis declares that the Marian interpretation is that of "some of the Fathers." From number 141 of *The True Devotion*, we see that Saint Louis is basing himself on at least two "Fathers": Origen and Saint Bonaventure; in his *Notebook*, where the same thought is expressed, the same two names are found.[128]

It is not difficult to find the reference of Saint Bonaventure, although it is not to be seen in any connection with Psalm 87 but when the saint speaks about the children of Noemi, a figure of Mary: "The two children of Mary, however, are a man-God and a pure man; she is the mother of one corporally, the mother of the other spiritually."[129] It is, however, difficult to find the reference made by Origen. When he comments on this psalm, there is no mention of the spiritual maternity. Perhaps Saint Louis is referring to Origen's famous commentary on the *Ecce Mater Tua* where the idea of two children of Mary is found.[130] It is interesting to note, however, that when speaking about this text of Origen, Montfort is undoubtedly basing himself on J. Crasset who declared that such is the mind of Origen, giving no reference whatsoever.[131]

Again, although the text is no proof for the spiritual maternity, nonetheless, it does show us the strong conviction of Saint Louis that the inspired Word of God tells us that Mary is our Mother. It must also be remembered that these two Scripture texts are not central to Montfort's discussion concerning the spiritual maternity. The missionary could himself consider these texts as accommodations without weakening in the least his central proof for this prerogative, Mary's role as the Mother-Associate in the redemptive Incarnation.

4. *Luke 1:26-38.* The biblical narration of the Annunciation scene need not be cited in full here. The important words of this text, as far as the spiritual maternity is concerned, are the following: "Behold thou shalt conceive in thy womb and shalt bring forth a son; and thou shalt call His name Jesus. He shall be great and shall be called the Son of the Most High; and the Lord God will give Him the throne of David his Father and He shall be king over the house of Jacob forever and of His kingdom there shall be no end ... The Holy One to be born of thee shall be called the Son of God ... But Mary said, 'Behold the handmaid of the Lord, be it done to me according to thy word.'" We are interested here in discovering if Saint Louis de Montfort, from the very words of Scripture, deduces the spiritual maternity; how he reasons from the mystery of the Incarnation to this prerogative is another question.

Nowhere in the writings of Saint Louis does he explicitly state that the spiritual maternity is proved by the words of the Annunciation. However, at first sight, it would seem that he does give us a major and a minor for such a conclusion, for he tells us that: "by the Angelic Salutation, God became man, a virgin became the Mother of God, the souls of the just were delivered from Limbo, the empty thrones in heaven filled. In addition sin was forgiven, grace was given to us ..."[132] As we have already seen, in his *Cantiques*, he tells us "God redeemed the world by the 'Hail Mary.'"[133] Now, as Montfort tells us, Our Lady was chosen as His instrument for this tremendous event and it was put into effect when she was greeted with the Angelic Salutation.[134] Therefore, we may legitimately conclude, Mary is our Mother; for if Redemption began with the Incarnation and Mary has a necessary part in this mystery, then it is evident that she gives us spiritual birth. We could say, therefore, that Montfort would agree with the opinion of those Mariologists who declare that the spiritual maternity is found formally, though implicitly in the Lucan narration.[135]

But the question of Montfort's opinion is not so quickly solved. Are St. Louis' major and minor deduced precisely from the words of Scripture? Is it because of the text of Luke that Saint Louis declares that grace is given to us, that the thrones of heaven are filled, etc.? Or is it rather a deduction the missionary makes, not directly from the Scripture text, but from the general teaching of the Church on the nature of the Redemption and the Incarnation? If so—and from the context this appears more likely—then Lk. 1:26-38 is not an explicit proof in itself for the spiritual maternity. We may say that it becomes a proof for Montfort when he joins to it the nature of the redemptive Incarnation and the nature of Mary's role in this mystery. In other words, the spiritual maternity appears to be found in the Annuncation scene virtually, as far as Montfort is concerned.

5. *John 19:26-27.* The text of Saint John is well-known: "Jesus, therefore, seeing His Mother and the disciple whom He loved standing by, said to His Mother, Woman behold thy son. Then He said to the disciple, Behold thy Mother. And from that hour the disciple took her into his own." What is the opinion of Saint Louis concerning this text, used by most authors to prove the spiritual maternity? We are struck, first of all, by his almost total silence on this text. In none of his works dealing *ex professo* with Our Lady does he even mention the text, "Behold thy Mother." This should not surprise us, for as we have already seen, Montfort's Mariology is centered on the Redemptive Incarnation. Twice in his *True Devotion,* however, he does declare that those who give

themselves to Mary can say with Saint John: "I have taken her for my own"[136]—implying that Mary's spiritual maternity is somehow found in the Johannine text.

Montfort's thoughts on this text are explained principally in his small pamphlet, "Dispositions for a Happy Death," where we find comments on the seven last words of Our Lord. However, it appears that only the first part of this Leaflet is from the pen of St. Louis de Montfort. The section in question is taken from Father J. Nouet, S.J., (†1680).[137] The short work believed by many to be entirely written by Montfort was found among the few belongings of the missionary the eve of his death, and Father Mulot, one of the first members of his community, wrote in the blank spaces of the pamphlet the *Last Will and Testament* which the saint dictated to him from his death bed. We will quote from this section of the *Dispositions for a Happy Death*, understanding that at best, they represent thoughts concerning Jn. 19:26-27 which St. Louis appreciated.

Two sentences of Father Nouet concern the *Ecce Mater Tua*: "O Jesus, who when dying didst show the tenderness of thy Heart towards thy Mother and to her hath recommended all Thy disciples in the person of Saint John, place me, I pray, under her protection and give me a true heart of a son to honor her";[138] and the prayer to Our Lady which immediately follows: "O Mary, remember that thy Son from the tree of the Cross hath recommended to thee my soul; prove to Him that thou art a good Mother and that thou takest care of my salvation. *Monstra te esse Matrem*, Show thyself a Mother."[139] However, in his *Prayer for Missionaries*, Saint Louis explicitly includes his congregation in this text: "Be mindful, O Lord, of thy congregation ... which Thou hast possessed in thy heart when thy Son, dying on the Cross, sprinkled it with His blood and consecrated it with His death, confiding it to His Holy Mother."[140]

We would be led to believe, therefore, that Saint Louis

recognizes in this text more than a filial act on the part
of Our Lord, for in the person of Saint John, as Father
Nouet declares, all true disciples are included; Saint John
represents all Christians, the entire Church. We can then
tentatively conclude that Montfort does see in this text
the fact of Mary's Motherhood of all the faithful, her
Motherhood of the Church.

Although this Johannine text is commonly accepted by
Catholic scholars to refer in some way to Mary's spiritual
motherhood,[141] the missionary's few authentic (and rather
vague) references to this text prove to us that it is not
an important one in his teaching on the spiritual maternity.[142] Montfort considers this text, we would say, the
promulgation of the fact of Mary's motherhood of men,
a motherhood which has its origin not in these words, but
in the Incarnation, and its completion through the Cross-
Resurrection. Saint Louis insists, therefore, not on this
promulgation, but on the redemptive Incarnation, to deduce his doctrine of the spiritual maternity.[143]

B. Arguments from Tradition

Not only by Scripture, but also by arguments from tradition, does Saint Louis attempt to prove his thesis on the
spiritual maternity. He was well grounded in the doctrine
of the Fathers as understood in his day[144] and states in
his *True Devotion* that, were he not writing for the poor
and the simple, he would include many texts from the
Fathers of the Church.[145]

Nonetheless, Father de Montfort does use some arguments of the Fathers to uphold his thesis on the spiritual
maternity. We have already seen his insistence on Origen
and Bonaventure in the interpretation of Psalm 87. There
are three additional arguments used by Montfort from tradition: one general argument and two from Saint Augustine. We will examine each in detail.

1. *General Argument from the Fathers*

"Note that Mary is also the Mother of His (Christ's) members; that is the teaching of the Fathers of the Church."[146]

That Montfort is justified in invoking this tradition of the Church to deduce the prerogative of the spiritual maternity, there can be no doubt. Not only the brief historical survey given at the beginning of this work proves this point, but also the special studies which have been made on this subject. Beginning with Saint Irenaeus' theory on the New Eve, as Joseph Bover observes, the spiritual maternity is found throughout patristic literature,[147] although, as previously noted, the title "Mother of the Living" occurs only at the latter part of the fourth century in the writings of Saint Epiphanius. Jaime Garreta, in his study of this prerogative of Our Lady finds numerous quotations to prove his thesis that it was taught from the earliest times.[148] G. Joussard, although giving examples of the faith of the early Fathers of the Church in the spiritual maternity, is more restrained in his judgment concerning the first eight centuries of the Church.[149] William O'Connor, in his comparatively short article on the subject, cites approximately thirty Fathers of the Church in support of this tradition.[150] It would appear legitimate, therefore, to declare that the spiritual maternity is taught—although at times only implicitly—by the Fathers of the Church.[151]

Moreover, the precise argument alleged by Saint Louis, that the Fathers call Mary the Mother of the members of Christ, is also found in tradition. Saint Augustine, as we shall see shortly, is perhaps the first to mention explicitly this aspect of Mary's motherhood,[152] followed at least implicitly by Saint Leo the Great,[153] pseudo-Ambrose[154] and others.

Saint Louis de Montfort, acquainted with this tradition, can correctly point to it when declaring that Mary is truly the Mother of men.

2. *Arguments from Saint Augustine*

Saint Louis finds it impossible not to bring forward at least two testimonies of Saint Augustine to prove this tradition of the Fathers, both of which are not without their difficulties. We will, therefore, consider both citations in detail.

a. "The Elect are in the Womb of Mary"

"Saint Augustine, surpassing himself and everything that I have just said, says that all the predestinate, in order to be conformed to the image of the Son of God, are in this world, hidden in the womb of the Blessed Virgin, where they are guarded, nourished, brought up and made to grow by that good Mother until she has brought them forth to glory after death, which is properly the day of their birth."[155] This text pleases Montfort so much that it is repeated throughout his works: "Saint Augustine says that the elect are in the womb of Mary and that she only brings them forth when they enter into glory."[156] "Saint Augustine even says that in this world the predestinate are all enclosed in the womb of Mary and that they are not born until this good Mother brings them forth to eternal life."[157] The text of Augustine, as presented by Saint Louis, is undoubtedly a firm assertion of the fact of Mary's spiritual maternity; she is portrayed as the Woman spiritually pregnant with the human race.

Such a text, however, can be found nowhere in the writings of the great doctor of Hippo; nor can it even be located in the apocryphal works under his name.

Where did Saint Louis find this text? We must recall that much of his study of the Fathers appears to be second-hand; for the most part, he read the works of the Fathers as they are cited and explained in various authors like F. Poiré, L. D'Argentan, J. Crasset and others. We do find this text of Augustine in Poiré's writings—which Montfort placed in his *Notebook*: "I base myself on a

rich conception of the great Saint Augustine, who in his
book on Holy Virginity, having said that the Blessed Virgin is our Mother by spirit and by grace, as she is of the
Savior by nature, he carries this thought even further and
notes that she is delivered of her children when she gives
them birth for heaven: consequently that she carries
them in her womb ('*flancs*') as long as they are here below, awaiting a better condition."[158]

Poiré refers to Saint Augustine's *De Sacra Virginitate.*
The text he is alluding to is probably the well known,
"Mother indeed in spirit not of our head ... but clearly
mother of His members which we are; for she has cooperated by charity so that the faithful, who are members of the Head, may be born in the Church; corporally,
however, she is the mother of the Head."[159] Firstly, it
must be noted that this text of Saint Augustine is at most
a doubtful proof for this prerogative of Our Lady. For
in its context, we see that Saint Augustine is attributing
to Mary a spiritual maternity equal to that which a virgin can have by her charity. As E. Neubert has declared,
although the text appears so clear, the context shows that
Augustine is not speaking about the special spiritual maternity which is Our Lady's.[160]

However, even granted that this text of Saint Augustine
does refer to the spiritual maternity, where does he declare
in this text that all Christians are contained in the womb
of Mary? The thought would appear to be taken from
Saint Augustine's (apocryphal) *De Symbolo ad Catechumenos* where calling Mary a figure of the Church, he declares that the Church conceives us in its womb at baptism
and gives us birth when we enter into paradise.[161] The application, therefore, to Mary is easily made; however,
such an application is not made by the author of *De
Symbolo,* and surely not by Saint Augustine.

This text of Augustine as given by Saint Louis de Montfort—which he evidently took from Poiré—is a compila-
tion of two texts of Augustine, one apocryphal, the other

doubtfully referring to the spiritual maternity. Although it does present to us a powerful insight of Montfort into the nature of the spiritual maternity, we cannot consider it as the opinion of the holy doctor of Hippo.

b. "The Mold of God"

There is, however, another text of Augustine which Saint Louis employs when speaking about the spiritual maternity. "Saint Augustine calls Our Lady the mold of God—the mold fit to cast and mold gods. He who is cast in this mold is presently formed and molded in Jesus Christ and Jesus Christ in him."[162] The same thought is found in the *Secret of Mary,* number 16. The Sulpician, M. Tronson, is Montfort's source for this argument: "She has become a mold of God: *forma Dei,* says St. Augustine."[163] For Tronson as for St. Louis, this expression does not imply a passive attitude on the part of the Christian; rather, with the grace of God, man is to actively cooperate in his transformation into the life of Christ.

The text to which Saint Louis refers—"*Si formam Dei appellem, digna existis*"[164]—is found in the apocryphal sermon 208 attributed to Saint Augustine. It is true that in the preceding verse, pseudo-Augustine calls Mary *matrem gentium,* but Montfort makes no mention of this verse. Basing himself solely on the fact that 'Augustine' calls Mary the 'mold of God' because she has given birth to the God-Man, Saint Louis reasons that it is she also who forms us in God by grace. The reasoning is not found in pseudo-Augustine. It is, evidently, no argument from tradition but rather another way that Montfort repeats a favorite thought: Mary cooperates in our redemption at the Incarnation, therefore in some mysterious way her efficacious *fiat* perdures for all eternity and she is rightfully called, the Mother of men.

C. *Theological Arguments*

That Mary is the Mother of men is most strongly asserted by Saint Louis when he discusses the theological reasons why God the Son wills that she 'incarnate' Him in the elect. Basing himself on the truth that Mary is the Mother-Associate of God the Redeemer—his prime principle of Mariology—Saint Louis concludes to the spiritual maternity. We will, for the sake of clarity, first consider Mary as the Companion of the Redeemer, then as Mother of the Redeemer, to understand how Montfort deduces the spiritual maternity from this basic prerogative of Mary.

✠   ✠   ✠

1. THE COMPANION OF THE REDEEMER[165]

Our Lady has, with Christ and subordinately to Him, cooperated in the redemption of the human race, thereby enabling man to enjoy God's loving presence and to be transformed into this presence. She has, therefore, cooperated in our spiritual birth and can rightly be called "Our Mother." Thus can the argument from 'consortship' be summarized, which Saint Louis succinctly states when he declares: "You (Our Lady) give us life, because you break our chains."[166] The full import of these words, the complete thought of Saint Louis on this point can only be grasped after having studied Montfort's writings concerning the union of Jesus and Mary in the work of the redemption in general and then as shown in the Incarnation and the Sacrifice of Calvary.

a. *The Union of the Redeemer and Our Lady.* Saint Louis' constant insistence on the doctrine of the 'consortship' is known to anyone who is even slightly acquainted with any one of his writings. Jesus and Mary are united, by the will of the Father, in the work of redemption.[167] This principle is clearly enunciated in number 74 of his *True Devotion*: "Jesus Christ chose her (Mary) for the inseparable companion of His life, of His death, of His glory and of His power in heaven and earth."[168] This

union begins at the moment of the Incarnation, for Montfort sings of this mystery: "They (Jesus and Mary) appear fused together. How beautiful is the alliance! Mary
is all in Jesus ... or better still, she is no longer but only
Jesus in her."[169]

So intense is this union that the Saint tries to search for
words which can adequately express this alliance of Jesus
and Mary: "They are so intimately united that one is altogether in the other. Jesus is altogether in Mary and Mary
is altogether in Jesus; or rather, she exists no more but
Jesus alone in her and it were easier to separate the light
from the sun than Mary from Jesus, so that we may call
Our Lord, Jesus of Mary and Our Blessed Lady, Mary of
Jesus."[170] Saint Louis' insight into this *sociatio* of the Redeemer and Mary makes him cry out. "I turn here for one
moment to Thee, O sweet Jesus, to complain lovingly to thy
Divine Majesty that the greater part of Christians, even
the most learned, do not know the necessary union there is
between Thee and Thy Holy Mother. Thou, Lord, art always with Mary and Mary is always with Thee and she
cannot be without Thee else she would cease to be what
she is ... She is so intimately united with Thee that it were
easier to separate the light from the sun, the heat from
the fire, it were easier to separate from Thee all the angels
and saints than the divine Mary";[171] wherever Jesus is,
He is the fruit of Mary.[172]

From these few texts of Saint Louis we can see his
constant insistence on Mary as the Associate of the Redeemer, from the moment of the Incarnation, through all
the events of His Life, through the Cross-Resurrection and
even now in eternal glory. A woman of this earth, the
representative of all the redeemed, has been chosen, according to Montfort, to be the intimate associate of the
Lord Jesus Christ, the Wisdom of the Father, in his work
of transforming this universe into Himself; through the
divinely-willed cooperation of Mary, the day will come
when this entire universe will be in the power of the Spirit,

one in Christ to the eternal praise of the Father.

The Second Vatican Council insisted strongly upon this principle of consortship: "Mary, the Mother of God, who is joined by an inseparable bond to the saving work of her Son";[173] "The Blessed Virgin was eternally predestined, in conjunction with the incarnation of the divine Word, to be the Mother of God. By decree of divine Providence, she served on earth as the loving mother of the divine Redeemer, an associate of unique nobility and the Lord's humble handmaid. . . . in an utterly singular way she cooperated by her obedience, faith, hope and burning charity in the Savior's work of restoring supernatural life to souls. For this reason she is a mother to us in the order of grace";[174] "she devoted herself totally as a handmaid of the Lord to the person and work of her Son";[175] "united to Him by a close and indissoluble tie, she is endowed with the supreme office and dignity of being the Mother of the Son of God";[176] "Mary figured profoundly in the history of salvation . . ."[177]

Pope Paul, in *Marialis Cultus,* also insists on Mary as the "Associate of the Redeemer";[178] and speaks of the "indissoluble link and essential relationship of the Virgin to the Divine Savior."[179] One of the points of agreement between the Catholic and non-Catholic theologians at the International Marian Congress in Rome, May 1975, included the statement: "God wanted to associate in various degrees to the work of Redemption the created collaborators, among whom the Virgin Mary has an exceptional dignity and efficacy."[180]

This union of Jesus and Mary is accentuated by Saint Louis and explained more fully by him when he speaks about the Redemptive Incarnation and the Sacrifice of the Cross.

b. *The Union of the Redeemer and Our Lady at the Incarnation.* It is especially at the Incarnation that Saint Louis sees Mary as the companion of the Redeemer, with

Christ and subordinately to Him, cooperating in the re-demption of the world. Before considering Mary's role in this mystery, we will first see the nature of the Incarna-tion according to Montfort, the better to understand the part he attributes to Mary.

Having declared the Incarnation the principal mystery of his devotion,[181] it is not surprising that Montfort de-velops the nature of this mystery throughout his writings. It will suffice here to demonstrate that in Montfort's eyes there is an insistence that the Incarnation is redemptive; if Our Lady shares in this mystery, she also, therefore, shares some way in the redemption by which supernatural life has been won.

There is no difficulty in showing that Montfort insists on the redemptive character of the Incarnation. The pur-pose of the Incarnation is to redeem mankind: "The Eternal Wisdom, having decided, in the great council of the Trinity, to become man in order to restore fallen man, He made this known to Adam, as we can believe, and promised to the ancient Patriarchs, as Holy Scripture de-clares, that He would become man to redeem the world."[182] Montfort preached to his people, the simple folk of western France at the beginning of the 18th century, that we must not consider redemption to be limited to the death of Christ on Calvary, for redemption 'begins' at the Incarna-tion, we have been redeemed by the 'Hail Mary.' In Saint Louis' commentary on the text of Hebrews 10:5-10[183] this is again clearly brought out: "My heart is ready, My God, My Father, to do your will; here in the womb of My Moth-er, I submit to it in truth. I adore you, I love you, here I am, dispose of me. I place in the center of myself your cross and your law. You make me see at this hour that it is necessary that I embrace the cross and that it is even necessary that I die upon it. I will it, My God, it is my choice."[184] The sacrifice of the Cross is then the culmina-tion of the sacrifice of Christ begun in the womb of Mary; and not only begun, but contained virtually: "It is in this

mystery (the Incarnation) that He has worked all the
mysteries of his life which have followed, by the acceptance
that He made of them: *Jesus ingrediens mundum dixit:
Ecce venio ut faciam Deus, voluntatem tuam* ... This mystery is then the abridgement of all mysteries and contains
the will and the grace of all."[185] Montfort, therefore, attributes to the Incarnation itself, the effects of the Redemption.[186]

It is interesting to note that Pope Paul VI declares in
Marialis Cultus: "With regard to Christ, the East and
the West, in the inexhaustible riches of their liturgies,
celebrate this solemnity (the Annunciation) as the commemoration of the salvific 'fiat' of the Incarnate Word,
who entering the world said: "God, here I am! I am
coming to obey your will" (cf. Heb 10:7, Ps 39:8-9). They
commemorate it as the beginning of the redemption and of
the indissoluble and wedded union of the divine nature
with human nature in the one Person of the Word";[187]
"As a Gospel prayer, centered on the mystery of the redemptive Incarnation, the Rosary is therefore a prayer
with a clearly Christological orientation."[188] Pope Paul explicitly speaks of the "redemptive Incarnation," the "salvific fiat," the "salvific dialogue," including the Annunciation as a "salvific episode."

Saint Louis insists on this redemptive character of the
mystery of the Incarnation: if he considers Mary as having a part in this mystery, then, in his opinion, she has
contributed to the redemption of the human race and, as we
have seen, continually cooperates with Christ in the spiritual transformation of men.

Saint Louis de Montfort considers Mary's role as Associate of the Redeemer in the Incarnation, principally under
two aspects which we should briefly consider: Mary has
'merited' the Incarnation and she has consented to the
proposal of the Incarnation.

Mary's cooperation in the redemption at the moment of
the Incarnation is described by Montfort, first of all, by

declaring that she merited the Incarnation, while the patriarchs of the Old Testament could not: "their cries, their
prayers and their sacrifices of their hearts ... were not of
a great enough price to merit this grace of graces."[189] Yet,
the missionary boldly declares: "There was found only
Mary who by the sublimity of her virtue attained to the
very throne of the Divinity and has merited this infinite
treasure"[190] ... "it was only Mary who merited it (the
Incarnation) and found grace before God by the force of
her prayers and the eminence of her virtues."[191] Saint
Louis, therefore, clearly states that the patriarchs could
not merit the Incarnation, yet Mary, because of her holiness, has merited it, thereby sharing in our redemption.

In the language of his day, and following his sources,
it would appear that Montfort is speaking about the hastening of the Incarnation, not in any way declaring that
Mary truly merited the Incarnation itself. The prophets
and patriarchs prayed for his coming but could not bring
the Incarnation to occur in their time, so Montfort would
declare; but Mary, never considered an independent agent
by Montfort, but because of the free gift of her sublime
holiness (Montfort insists on the Immaculate Conception)
had her prayers answered, her prayers for the coming of
Yahweh, for the Day of the Lord. Actually, Montfort is
speaking here about the gift of holiness given by God to
Mary, a gift so intense that her prayers for the coming
of the Lord were answered. Saint Louis sees in these
prayers of Mary, answered because of her God-given holiness, a cooperation in the redemptive Incarnation.

However, when considering Mary's cooperation in the
redemption at the moment of the Incarnation, Montfort
insists not so much on Mary's meriting the hastening of
the coming of the Lord, but on the efficacy of her *fiat*.
It is through her "Yes" that the redemptive Incarnation
took place. Her consent was, Montfort insists, necessary
—by the will of God—so that God would become man, the
Savior of the world: "The Eternal Wisdom desired to

become man in her, provided that she give her consent."[192] Mary's consent was therefore necessary in God's plan; nonetheless, it was not a forced consent, but depended upon her free will: "This salutation was *presented* to terminate the most important affair of the world, the Incarnation of the Eternal Word"[193] and as we have just seen, God would become man "provided that" she consent; therefore, Montfort is insisting on her loving freedom at the moment of the annunciation. In fact, Montfort calls this consent of Mary an act of supernatural love based upon pure faith by which she voluntarily accepted whatsoever this consent would entail.[194]

According to Saint Louis, Mary's consent is, therefore, truly efficacious for the redemption of the entire human race, to such an extent that we can speak of grace as "*materna.*" She speaks for all mankind yearning for redemption, and in the name of mankind, lovingly consents to God's plan that Divine Wisdom become one of us, while remaining fully God. When we keep in mind Montfort's conception of the nature of the Incarnation, all the more important does this consent of Our Lady appear; truly by it she cooperates in our redemption, for her necessary *fiat* is for Montfort efficacious throughout all eternity (she is the Redeemer's associate even in His glory!). Montfort has no hesitation, therefore, in concluding that Mary is the Mother of all mankind.

Montfort's teaching concerning Mary's role at the Incarnation is strikingly reflected in Paul VI's *Marialis Cultus*: "the Blessed Virgin's free consent and cooperation in the plan of redemption";[195] "one perceives how through the assent of the humble Handmaid of the Lord mankind begins its return to God";[196] "Mary, who taken into dialogue with God, gives her active and responsible consent, not to the solution of a contingent problem, but to that 'event of world importance' as the Incarnation of the Word has been rightly called";[197] "These liturgies celebrate it (the Annunciation) as a culminating moment in the salvific dialogue between God and man and as a commemoration of the Blessed Virgin's free consent and cooperation in the plan of redemption."[198] The words of Pope Paul echo the Second Vatican Council: "The maternity of Mary in the order of grace began with the consent which she gave in faith at the Annunciation";[199] "In subordination to Him and along with Him, by the grace of almighty God she served the mystery of redemption. Rightly therefore the holy Fathers see her as used by God not merely in a passive way, but as cooperating in the work of human salvation through free faith and obedience."[200] The American Bishops' Pastoral Letter on Mary declares: "The chapter on Mary in the Dogmatic Constitution on the Church may be regarded as an extended commentary on her consent at the Annunciation."[201]

Because of Mary's *fiat* at the moment of the annunciation, Saint Louis calls Mary a victim with Jesus from the moment of the Incarnation: "Their hearts, united very strongly by intimate ties, are offered both together to be two victims, in order to hold back the chastisement which our crimes merit."[202] Mary is, therefore, the associate of the redeemer at the Incarnation and Saint Louis can, therefore, deduce the spiritual maternity from this fact, declaring: "In this mystery, the elect have received their birth. Mary, united with Jesus, chose them in advance to have part in their virtues, their glory and their power";[203] "it is in this mystery that Jesus, together with Mary . . . chose all the elect."[204]

c. *The Union of the Redeemer and Our Lady at Calvary.*
Mary is the associate of the redeemer. Montfort speaks of this fact not only when considering the Incarnation, but also when he considers the sacrifice of Christ on Calvary. It is interesting that nowhere in his writings does the missionary explicitly deduce the spiritual maternity from Mary's cooperation in the sacrifice of the Cross; this is found only implicitly in his writings. His insistence is on

Mary's cooperation—by her loving, free consent—to the Incarnation itself.

Nonetheless, although not explicitly deducing the spiritual maternity from Mary's association with the Redeemer at the Cross, Montfort does strongly insist on Our Lady's cooperation in the sacrifice of Christ.[205] And there are several ways that Mary does show herself to be the associate of Christ in his sacrifice. Following the theological pattern of his age, Saint Louis speaks of Mary's cooperation under the aspects of redemption, satisfaction and merit.

Mary has redeemed us with and subordinately to Christ, because she has, according to Montfort, relinquished her maternal rights over her Victim Son, willingly offering Him for the redemption of the human race. This principle is clearly expressed by Saint Louis when he tells us of the dependence of Jesus upon Mary, as a Son upon His Mother, in all the phases of His life, including His sacrificial death: "He has glorified his independence and His Majesty in depending on this admirable Virgin, in his conception, in his birth and his presentation in the temple, in his hidden life of thirty years, up to his death, where she had to assist, in order that He make with her but one and the same sacrifice and in order to be immolated by her consent to the Eternal Father as Isaac of old (was offered) by Abraham's consent to the will of God."[206] This thought is again expressed clearly by Saint Louis: "It is she who nursed Him, nourished Him, supported Him, raised and sacrificed Him for us."[207] This well-known text of Saint Louis clearly shows that Mary took part in what is called the formal element of the redemption, i.e., Jesus' willing acceptance of His death, for this act was accomplished with the consent of His Associate, Mary. In Montfort's thought, this is but the explicitation of the all-embracing consent which Mary already gave at the moment of the Incarnation.

The Second Vatican Council also speaks of Mary's cooperation with the Redeemer at Calvary: "The union of the Mother with the Son in the work of salvation was manifested from the time of Christ's virginal conception up to his death";[208] "There (at Calvary) she united herself with a maternal heart to His sacrifice and lovingly consented to the immolation of this Victim which she herself had brought forth";[209] "United with Him in suffering as He died upon the Cross."[210] The same thought is found clearly enunciated in *Marialis Cultus*: "The active love she showed ... on Golgotha";[211] "(Mary's) maternal role was extended and became universal on Calvary."[212] The American Bishops declared in their Pastoral Letter on Our Lady: "... Our Lady's fiat at the Annunciation was consummated in her total surrender to the Father's will at the foot of the cross ..."[213] And the Catholic and non-Catholic theologians at the Rome Marian Congress of 1975 agreed that "5. The cooperation of Mary was shown particularly when she believed in the Redemption, accomplished by her Son and when she remained at the foot of the Cross while almost all the Apostles ran away."[214]

Mary's participation in what is termed the material element of the redemption, the actual sufferings and death of Our Lord, is presented by Saint Louis when he speaks about the intense sufferings of Our Lady caused by the Passion of her Son and offered for the human race.[215] So strong do these expressions of Montfort appear concerning the association of Jesus and Mary in the work of redemption, that some theologians have declared that they believe that Montfort is implicitly insisting that Mary has cooperated proximately and immediately in the redemption.[216]

All we can say for certain is that, for Montfort, Mary's cooperation in the redemption is founded upon her efficacious consent to the Incarnation, which, for the saint, intimately and uniquely involves Mary in the salvation of mankind.

According to Saint Louis, Mary's cooperation in the redemption was accomplished to satisfy for the sins of men: "Sinners, we make by our crimes two innocent victims of Mary and Jesus,"[217] and as we have already seen, Montfort calls Jesus and Mary two victims, in order to hold back the wrath of God caused by our crimes.[218] The missionary can, therefore, call us "the glorious conquest of Jesus Christ crucified on Calvary, in union with his blessed Mother."[219] Mary's loving consent to the Incarnation, accepting all that her role would entail, appears to be the root of these expressions of Montfort concerning her participation in the sacrifice of her Son.

Nowhere in his writings does Saint Louis explicitly declare the exact nature of the 'merits' of Mary for the human race. He does, as we have seen when we considered Our Lady's plenitude of grace, often speak of Mary giving us of her merits, showing us that in some mysterious way, grace is 'maternalized' through her cooperation in the redemptive work; all grace is a *gratia materna* because of her association with Christ the Redeemer. This efficacious influence which Our Lady exercises in the redemption of the world because of the will of God and which has its roots in her role in the Incarnation gives Montfort the right to say to Mary: "You give us life because you break our chains."[220]

It gives him the right to conclude that in the strict sense of the term, she is the Mother of all men, the Mother of all Christians. And since grace is of its very nature ecclesial, Montfort is equivalently telling us that she is truly the Mother of the Church.

Our Lady, is therefore, by her efficacious association with the Redeemer both at the Incarnation and at Calvary (remembering that for Montfort this association begins at the annunciation and is an eternal one), the spiritual mother of the members of Christ.[221]

✠   ✠   ✠

2. THE DIVINE MATERNITY—
MARY, MOTHER OF THE REDEEMER

The prime principle of Montfort's Mariology is that
Mary is the Mother-Associate of God the Redeemer. As
we have seen, Saint Louis does deduce the spiritual maternity from the aspect of Mary's consortship; however,
it appears that even greater stress is placed upon the fact
that she is the Mother of God the Redeemer, when the
missionary speaks of the spiritual maternity. We can distinguish in Montfort's writings a double argument based
upon Mary's role as Mother of the Redeemer: Mary is
the Mother of the Savior who has redeemed us; and secondly, Mary is the Mother of the Head of the Mystical
Body. We will consider both these aspects as presented
to us by Saint Louis de Montfort.

a. *Mother of the Savior*

Our Lady has given a human nature to the Word of
God, the primary and only essential agent of our spiritual
regeneration; she is therefore our Mother. This argument
is found several times in the saint's writings, principally
in his *Cantiques*: "She has given us by her Son, both grace
and glory, life to the dead ...";[222] "You give us life in
giving us the fruit of Life";[223] "You give us life in giving
us this amiable Savior."[224] This would also appear to be
the sense of the words of the *Secret of Mary*: "Mary gave
being and life to the Author of all grace and that is why
she is called the Mother of Grace."[225]

It would appear, therefore, that Saint Louis recognizes
that Mary is the Mother of men because she is the Mother
of the Savior who gives us life. As such—and therefore
taken out of the context of Montfort's writings—it does
not conclude to a strict maternity, for her action is considered as terminating at the Person who in turn generates our spiritual life. However, this is not the full idea
of Saint Louis, as we already know, and which becomes

more evident when we now study his argument for the spiritual maternity based upon the fact that Mary is the Mother of the Head of the Mystical Body.

b. *Mother of the Head of the Mystical Body*

Our Lady is Mother of the Head of the Mystical Body. However, in Christ, the Head, we are all mystically one. Mary is, therefore, our Mother. Thus may the argument based upon Mary's maternity of the Head of the Mystical Body be summed up. We will first cite Saint Louis' presentation of this argument and then examine the validity of this deduction.

"If Jesus Christ, the Head of Men, is born in her, the predestinate, who are members of this Head must also be born in her by a necessary consequence. The same mother does not give birth to the Head without the members nor to the members without the Head, otherwise it would be a monster in the order of nature; likewise, in the order of grace, the head and members are born of the same Mother and if a member of the Mystical Body, that is to say, the predestined, were born of any other mother than Mary, who has produced the Head, he would not be one predestined nor a member of Jesus Christ, but a monster in the order of grace."[226]

A parallel text is found in the *Secret of Mary*: "Because Mary has formed the Head of the predestined, who is Jesus Christ, she must also form the members of this Head who are the true Christians, for a mother does not form the Head without the members nor the members without the Head."[227] In his *Love of the Eternal Wisdom*, the missionary also declares: "Note that Mary, besides being the Mother of Jesus, the Head of all the elect, is also the Mother of all His members, so that she begets them, bears them in her womb and brings them forth to the glory of heaven by the graces of God which she imparts to them."[228]

This is, moreover, for Montfort, the ultimate reason why the Father and the Holy Spirit will to have children by Mary; they have given her the grace to be Mother of the Head, she therefore cooperates in the spiritual generation of all the members.[229]

Saint Louis is speaking directly about Our Lady's maternity of men in ongoing redemption, basing himself on the fact that she gave physical birth to the Head at the Incarnation and thereby gives spiritual birth to all His members.

Yet what is the value of this argument? Can it be said that Our Lady is the spiritual mother of men by the fact that she gives birth to the Head of the Mystical Body? C. Zimara does not hesitate to declare that this argument of Saint Louis de Montfort is absolutely nil in proving the spiritual maternity since it contains an illogical deduction from one order (Mother of Christ physically) to another (Mother of the members spiritually) ; at the very most, so he reasons, may it be called an argument of fittingness or suitability (*ratio convenientiae*).[230] On the other hand, E. Mura extols this argument as presented by Saint Louis as splendidly expressed, in conformity with the most solid, profound and traditional teaching of Christian dogma.[231] What is the value of this argument of Saint Louis?

Extrinsically, first of all, we are led to believe that it is a valid premise for the spiritual maternity, for practically all authors treating of this prerogative of Our Lady include a similar argument. Moreover, this argument of Saint Louis de Montfort was, as E. Mura declares, given weight and authority when St. Pius X included it in his encyclical *Ad diem illum*.[232] Since the Holy Father depended upon Montfort for this argument, we would consider it important to quote his words: "For is not Mary the Mother of Christ? She is therefore our Mother also. Indeed, everyone must believe that Jesus the Word made flesh is also the Savior of the human race. Now as the God-Man he acquired a body composed like that of any other man, but as the Savior of our race He had a kind of spiritual and mystical Body which is the society of those who believe in Christ. 'We the many are one body in Christ' (Rom. 12:5). But the Virgin conceived the Eternal Son not only that He might be made man by taking His human nature from her but also that by means of that nature assumed from her, He might be the Savior of men. For this reason the angel said to the shepherds, 'Today in the town of David a Savior has been born to you who is Christ the Lord' (Luke 2:11). So in one and the same bosom of His most chaste Mother, Christ took to Himself human flesh and at the same time united to Himself the spiritual body built up of those who are to believe in Him. Consequently, Mary, bearing in her womb the Savior, may be said to have borne also all those whose life was contained in the life of the Savior. All of us, therefore, who are united with Christ and are as the Apostle says, 'Members of His body, made from His flesh and from His bones' (Eph. 5:30) have come forth from the womb of Mary as a body united to its head. Hence in a spiritual and mystical sense, we are called children of Mary and she is the Mother of us all."[233]

These words of Pius X are equivalently restated not only by Pius XII,[234] but also by Pope Paul VI: "In the mystery of Mary's Motherhood they confess that she is the Mother of the Head and of the Members ..."[235] The Bishops of the United States declared: "Physically mother of Christ the Head, Mary is spiritually mother of the members of Christ"[236] and again, "... the full understanding of Mary's motherhood of Jesus contains also the secret of her spiritual motherhood of the brethren of Christ."[237] The immediate source of the statements of Pope Paul in *Marialis Cultus* and of the American Bishops appears to be the Second Vatican Council, which, quoting Saint Augustine, declared: "Indeed she is 'clearly the mother of the members of Christ ... since she cooperated out of love so that there might be born in the Church the faithful, who are members of Christ their Head.' "[238]

Considering, therefore, theological authors and especially the encyclical of St. Pius X and later documents of the Church, it does appear that we can rightfully deduce the spiritual maternity from the fact that Mary has given birth to the Head of the Mystical Body.

This becomes even more evident when we consider the argument in itself. Saint Louis de Montfort bases himself on the unity of Head and Members of the Mystical Body and upon the role of Mary in the birth of this Head. We will, therefore, consider both these elements.

1) *The Union of Head and Members in the Mystical Body.*
The fact of the intimate union between the Head and the members of the Mystical Body is forcefully declared by Saint Paul: "As in one body we have many members ... so being many, we are one body in Christ."[239] Such also is the mind of tradition, summed up by Saint Thomas: "As a natural body is one, consisting of diversity of members, so the entire Church, which is the mystical Body of Christ, is considered as one person with its Head, who is Christ."[240] This same doctrine is forcefully taught by Pope Pius XII when he calls this union "most compact" (*arctissimam*)[241] and declares it to be the constant and ancient doctrine of the Fathers.[242]

But what is this intimate unity which connects Head and members? It is by all means more than a moral unity; by no means is it a substantial or hypostatic union. It is a unity which is termed "mystical" for the ultimate source of this oneness with the Head is found not in the order of nature but in the supernatural order of grace. We the members retain our own personality, our own natural subsistence, our own natural being, but as E. Mura states: "In the superior order, in the order of supernatural and divine life, He (Christ) forms with them (the members) the same mystical Person: it is the effect of His capital grace."[243] It is then ultimately because of the capital grace of Christ that we form but one Mystical Person, that Head and members are united to form

One Body and we are thereby one with Christ mystically.[244]

Since the Incarnation is, in the present order of things, essentially soteriological, we can say that the Redeemer's habitual grace, from the first moment of His existence in Mary's womb, was ordained to the sanctification of men; which is equivalent to saying that from the first moment of the Incarnation, Christ possessed this capital grace by which we form with Him but one Mystical Body.[245]

2) *The Role of Mary in this Mystery.* Yet what is the role which Our Lady plays in this union of Head and Members? If this oneness with Christ is ultimately accomplished by the capital grace of Christ, how can we speak of Mary having a part in this mystery? If, as Saint Louis declares, there is a "necessary consequence" from the maternity of the Head to the maternity of the members, in his opinion she must have some definite role to play in this union of Head and Members through the capital grace of Christ.

Although, as is evident, Our Lady has not given birth to the divine nature, nonetheless, her generative act terminates at the hypostatic union itself.[246] She is the *Theotokos*, the Mother of God. And by the very fact that she has supplied a human nature for the Word, this God-Man is necessarily head of the human race, even if we do not consider the question of capital grace. For in the hypothesis of an incarnation in a humanity free from sin, Christ would still be head of the human race by the first two manners mentioned by Saint Thomas, order and perfection.[247] However, Mary's spiritual maternity is in the order of grace, as is the ultimate reason for our incorporation in Christ; we are seeking, therefore, Mary's relationship to this union of Head and Members through the capital grace of Christ, possessed by Him from the first moment of His existence in Mary's womb and by which all mankind is, in principle, transformed into Him.

Saint Louis de Montfort, writing to the simple people of the towns and hamlets of western France at the beginning of the 18th century, does not go into theological detail concerning this crucial point. On the other hand, his thoughts concerning the relationship of Mary to this union of Head and members through Christ's capital grace are found implicitly throughout his writings.

✠   ✠   ✠

In order to understand why Montfort can speak of this "necessary consequence" of the birth of the members because she is the Mother of the Head, there are three teachings of the missionary we must keep in mind. First of all, he stresses that at the Annunciation, Mary speaks as the representative of the entire human race: "The Son of God became man for *our* salvation . . . but after having asked her consent."[248] It is a consent given by Mary for which the "entire universe was awaiting for so many centuries."[249] Montfort appears to be alluding to the famous text of Saint Thomas: "(Mary) consents (to the Incarnation) in the place of the entire human nature, so that there would be a certain spiritual matrimony between the Son of God and human nature."[250] For Saint Louis de Montfort, Mary, as he tells us in *The Love of Eternal Wisdom*, no. 203: "found grace before God . . . for the entire human race"; she embodies in herself all mankind awaiting redemption. All mankind, the entire cosmos, says "Yes" to God's Love, in her name.

Secondly, we must recall that Montfort insists that this consent to the Incarnation of the Word is efficacious, for it is necessary because of the Will of God. "He would become man, provided that she would give her consent . . . the ineffable consent which the Holy Trinity . . . awaited."[251] Saint Louis, therefore, makes the Incarnation—and according to his thinking, therefore the entire redemptive work for all time—truly hinge upon this free and loving consent of humanity given in and through Mary. Her consent plays an efficacious role in the Incarnation of the Eternal Wisdom, the Redeemer, and therefore plays an efficacious role in the redemption of men. As the Second Vatican Council declared: "The Father of Mercies willed that the consent of the predestined mother should precede the Incarnation, so that just as a woman contributed to death, so also a woman should contribute to life."[252] The first part of this important text is repeated by the American Bishops in *Behold Your Mother*, no. 55.

There is a final point to consider in order to understand why Saint Louis concludes to the motherhood of the members because of the motherhood of the Head. In Montfort's eyes, Mary's consent to the Incarnation is not a blind act in which she is merely the unknowing instrument of the Lord. Such an opinion goes contrary to every page of his writings. Saint Louis would have no part with those authors who appear to be making a clear dichotomy between what could be called the 'Mary of History' and the 'Virgin of Faith,' declaring against the constant teaching of the Church, that, without any foundation in historical reality, Mary is the sign, the personification of the believing Christian. Montfort insists, as the Church still emphatically does today, on the basic reality and fundamental authenticity of Mary's role in the Incarnation as depicted by the Scriptures. That the Lucan Annunciation scene is couched in literary forms found in the Old Testament (cf. Jg 13:2-5) and language borrowed directly from earlier inspired writings (cf. Zep 3:14-17), no one can deny (cf. *Behold Your Mother*, nos. 21-33). However, to conclude from this that Lk 1:26-38 is a total, although justifiable, fabrication is to confuse the literary instrument with the truth conveyed; and the Church has always insisted on the reality of the "active and responsible consent" (*Marialis Cultus*, no. 37) of Mary to the redemptive Incarnation.

Moreover, it is quite inconceivable that the early Christians, especially their leaders, would depict Mary in such a crucial role unless there was a foundation in reality for this claim. Saint Louis de Montfort has, therefore, the right and the evangelical mandate to proclaim that Mary's consent, active and responsible, is directed towards the coming into the world of the *savior* of men. When speaking of the necessary aspect of the cooperation of Mary in the Incarnation, he says: "The Word becomes flesh, the Eternal Wisdom becomes incarnate, God has become man without ceasing to be God; this Man-God is called Jesus Christ, that is to say, *Savior*."[253] Again, in the context of her necessary and free consent, he writes: "The Son of God became man *for our salvation*"[254] and again, "It was through Mary that the salvation of the world was begun . . ."[255] and even more strongly: "If He is the *savior* of the world, it is by her virginity, it is by her profound humility."[256]

As we have already seen in other texts cited, the missionary declares that we have been redeemed by the 'Hail Mary,' for her consent at the Annunciation is in the name of the entire human race, a consent necessary by the will of God, *a loving consent to the breaking forth into our history of God's redemptive Love*, a consent which, like her knowledge of the Person and role of her Son clarified and intensified with the years. As Pope Paul expresses it: ". . . Mary . . . the obedient and faithful Virgin, who with her generous fiat (cf. Lk 1:38) became, through the working of the Spirit, the Mother of God but also the true Mother of the living . . ."[257] and as it is succinctly put by the American Bishops: "By accepting the Annunciation, she became intimately associated with all the saving mysteries of Jesus' life, death and Resurrection."[258] The Second Vatican Council, quoting Saint Irenaeus, declares: "(Mary), being obedient, became the cause of salvation for herself and the whole human race."[259] One of the points of agreement between Catholic and non-Catholic theologians at the Rome Marian Congress of 1975, was: "4. The 'fiat' which preserves a permanent character, was a free consent of Mary for the divine maternity and therefore for our salvation."[260]

Karl Rahner puts this truth most beautifully: "The absolutely unique Yes of consent of the Blessed Virgin, which cooperated in determining the whole history of the world, is not a mere happening that has disappeared in the void of the past . . . She still utters her eternal Amen, her eternal Fiat, Let it be so, Let it be done, to all that God willed, to the whole great ordered plan of redemption, in which we all find place, built up on the foundation which is Christ."[261] And as he says in his prayer to Mary: "For our salvation you said Yes, for us you spoke your Fiat."[262]

Because of these three points which run throughout Montfort's writings (and upon which he bases his Marian spirituality) he can rightly declare that there is a necessary consequence from Mary's motherhood of the Head to the motherhood of the members, from Mary's cooperation in the Incarnation of the Divine Wisdom to her cooperation in the spiritual incarnation of the Incarnate and Risen Wisdom in the hearts of men. For we are all one, at the moment of the Incarnation, with our Head, Jesus Christ; He is endowed with capital grace from the moment of His conception in Mary's womb. And this oneness with our Redeemer, God permitted to hinge on the faith-filled consent of a woman who represents the entire universe yearning for salvation. Like the Second Vatican Council, so too, Montfort's insights into the spiritual maternity are fundamentally a theological commentary on Mary's consent at the Incarnation.

Montfort can, therefore, rightfully conclude that Mary is our Mother since she is the Mother of the Head of the Mystical Body. Through her necessary cooperation in the redemptive Incarnation, a cooperation which continues for all eternity, she plays an efficacious role in our transformation into Christ and is, therefore, in the strict sense of the term, our Mother, our *Genetrix* in the order of grace.

✠   ✠   ✠

From these arguments of Scripture, tradition and theological reasoning, it appears that Saint Louis de Montfort has well proven his statement that the Wisdom of the Father wishes to form Himself and, so to speak, incarnate Himself in his members, through Mary. He has proven the prerogative of Our Lady's spiritual maternity. We find in his writings arguments not couched in the language of the university professor, but in the simple, metaphorical and often florid style of the missionaries of his age. However, piercing through the language of his day, it is apparent that for Montfort, the fact that Mary is our Mother is grounded on the firm rock of dogmatic truth and it was thus that he presented it to his people, in their own language, in their own thought patterns.

Although to be studied in some detail in another work, we can already see that the consequences of Saint Louis de Montfort's doctrine on the spiritual maternity are overwhelming. He sees this entire universe "in the womb of Mary." Taking all his writings into account, we can say that he implies by this that he sees this cosmos charged with the power of the Risen Lord drawing all things to Himself; but it is a power which has for Montfort, a maternal quality, it bears the imprint of Mary's eternal cooperation with God in the redemption of men. Because of her loving, efficacious consent to the Incarnation given in the name of the entire universe, her *fiat* resounds throughout eternity, cooperating in the transformation of this universe into the Risen Christ.

Montfort can, therefore, speak of living 'in Mary,' recognizing that this world and all humanity are forever being influenced by this woman. This is his 'secret,' this is his 'short way to perfection,' for it is but the recognition of the redemption of this world as God has willed it. These thoughts find strong expression on the lips of the missionary: "The predestinate are hidden in Mary's womb and they are not born until this good Mother brings them forth to eternal life";[263] "true children of Mary, engendered and conceived by her charity, carried in her womb, attached to her breasts, nourished with her milk, upheld by her arms, enriched by her graces, raised by her care";[264] "my womb gives you birth, it is I who engender you."

Mary is, therefore, our *Genetrix*. She does not merely act towards us like a mother, she does not merely take care of us because we have been legally placed in her charge, but with Christ and subordinately to Him, she is efficaciously and lovingly cooperating in our incorporation into our Final Goal, the Risen Christ, the Eternal and Incarnate Wisdom. We are truly the fruit of her womb.

CONCLUSION

Saint Louis de Montfort has been called the "Doctor of the Spiritual Maternity."[266] We hope that this overview of the foundations of Mary's motherhood of men according to Montfort proves the legitimacy of this title. He not only lived a life of filial devotion to the Mother of God but founded this prerogative of Mary on solid theological grounds and preached it in a simple but powerful way to the people of western France. Moreover, he did this when the cold of Jansenism was creeping over France and when Mariology was yet in its infancy. As Pope Pius XII declared of his doctrine so we can especially say of his teaching on the foundations of the spiritual maternity: it is *"flagrans, solida ac recta."*[267]

We must also conclude that the spiritual maternity, far from being forgotten by Saint Louis de Montfort, is one of the mainstays of his Sapiential spirituality. When the missionary, therefore, speaks of 'slave,' it is apparent that he is not opposing it to 'child,' but expressing the loving abandonment of a child to its mother who has given it birth. And if Our Lady is for Montfort, "Queen of All Hearts," it is but to express her maternal rights and privileges—her influence—over the hearts of her children.

The study of the foundations of the spiritual maternity according to Saint Louis de Montfort also gives us a better insight into the meaning of his "Total Consecration" for which he is so noted. Understanding that this consecration advocated by Montfort is directed ultimately to Jesus, the Eternal and Incarnate Wisdom, Mary also becomes the object of "consecration," precisely as our spiritual mother. The Montfortian consecration, therefore, is the formal recognition of an already established fact: Jesus the Eternal and Incarnate Wisdom is our Redeemer, and Mary is truly our spiritual mother. Interestingly enough, Montfort's sources, especially Cardinal de Bérulle, insist on Mary's universal sovereignty as the motive for 'consecration' or 'holy slavery.' Saint Louis de Montfort, however, insists on the spiritual maternity, which gives an entirely new aspect to the 'consecration' and 'holy slavery.' That is one of the reasons why the saint could so boldly declare: "But after all, I loudly protest, that having read nearly all the books which profess to treat of devotion to Our Lady and having conversed familiarly with the best and wisest men in these latter times, I have never known nor heard of any practice of devotion toward her at all equal to the one which I now wish to unfold."[268] Saint Pius X, recognizing the beauty and solidity of the Montfortian consecration, went so far as to grant a plenary indulgence *in perpetuum* to those who recite St. Louis' formula of consecration.

There is something quite mysterious about the writings of Saint Louis de Montfort. The initial reaction to his works—at least for many—would coincide with that of the Promoter of the Faith who (as mentioned in note 65 of part one), in 1853 scrutinized the writings of Montfort in view of his proposed beatification: "the devotion which the pious author proposes and upholds ... could never be approved by the Church; ... every sign of approbation or commendation of this writing must be avoided by all means." However, as Father Faber tells us: "I would venture to warn the reader that one perusal will be very far from making him the master of it (*The True Devotion*). If I may dare to say so, there is a growing feeling of something inspired and supernatural about it as we go on studying it; and with that we cannot help experiencing that its novelty never seems to wear off, nor its fulness to be diminished, nor the fresh fragrance and sensible fire of its unction ever to abate."[269] Theologians, bishops, popes, have agreed with Father Faber.[270]

From this brief study of the fact and the premises of the spiritual maternity according to the doctrine of Saint

Louis de Montfort, we can conclude with R. Bernard: "Of all the great spiritual writers of the last centuries, Louis Grignion de Montfort is, without contradiction, the one who has contributed the most towards impressing upon us this sentiment of our dependence on the Blessed Virgin and her maternity with regard to us."[271]

FOOTNOTES

INTRODUCTION

[1] "Ayant lu presque tous les livres qui traitent de la dévotion à la très sainte Vierge, et ayant conversé familièrement avec les plus grands saints et savants personnages de ces derniers temps..." (*V.Dév.*, no. 118).

[2] Cf. R. Laurentin, Court Traité de Théologie Mariale, (Paris, 1953) p. 113.
In the Marian bibliography of Father Besutti (G. M. Besutti, *Bibliographia Mariana*, Rome, 1968), which covers the years 1958-1966, seven thousand more titles are listed; however, since 1966, the quantity of Marian literature has decreased sharply.

[3] Cf. S. Justinus, *Dialogus cum Triphone, P.G.*, Vol. 6, 710.
For a detailed listing of Marian quotes from the Fathers of the Church, cf. Sergius Avarez Campos, O.F.M., *Corpus Marianum Patristicum*, 3 vols. (Burgos, 1970); cf. G. Jouassard, *Maternité Spirituelle: Première Tradition*, in *Bulletin Français d'Etudes Mariales*, Vol. 16 (1959), pp. 55-85; H. Barré, *La Maternité Spirituelle de Marie dans la Pensée Médiévale*, (*ibid*), pp. 87-118.

[4] Cf. S. Irenaeus, *Adversus Haereses*, Lib. 3, cap. 22, *P.G.* Vol. 7 958.

[5] Cf. Origenes, *In Evangelium Johannis*, I, Praefatio 6, *P.G.* Vol. 14, 32.

[6] Cf. S. Epiphanius, *Adversus Haereses*, 3, 2, *P.G.*, Vol. 42, 728-729.

[7] "Mater spiritu non Capitis nostri... sed plane Mater membrorum ejus" (S. Augustinus, *De Sancta Virginitate*, 6, *P.L.*, Vol. 40, 399).

[8] Cf. S. Germanus Constantinopolitanus, *Encomium in Beatam Virginem*, 3, *P.G.*, Vol. 86 (2), 3287.

[9] W. O'Connor, *The Spiritual Maternity of Our Lady in Tradition*, in *Marian Studies*, Vol. III (1952), p. 154.

[10] Cf. S. Anselmus, *Oratio 52, P.L.*, Vol. 158, 956.

[11] Cf. B. Morineau, S.M.M., *Comment la Doctrine de la Maternité*

Spirituelle de Marie s'installe dans la théologie mystique de S. Bernard, in *BEM,* Vol. I (1935) pp. 119 ff; cf. J. Canal, *La idea de la maternidad espiritual en San Bernardo,* in *Estudios Marianos,* 14 (1954) pp. 271-311.

[12] Cf. S. Aelredus, *Sermo 20, P.L.,* Vol. 195, 323.

[13] Cf. Rupert Tuitiensis, *In Evangelium S. Johannis,* 13, *P.L.,* Vol. 169, 789-790.

[14] S. Albertus Magnus, *Mariale,* qq. 11, 43, 166, etc.

[15] A prayer is attributed to St. Thomas which calls Mary 'mater omnium credentium' but is of doubtful authenticity. Cf. W. O'Connor, *art. cit.,* p. 163; G. Roschini, *La Mariologia di San Tommaso,* (Roma, 1950), p. 163.

[16] Cf. *S.Th.* III, q. 28, a. 1; For other references, see G. Roschini, *op. cit.,* pp. 163 ff.

[17] Cf. S. Bonaventura, *Sermo 26, In Nativitate Domini,* in *Opera Omnia,* Vol. 9 (Ad Claras Aquas, 1901), p. 125.

[18] Cf. L. di Fonzo, O.F.M. Conv., *La mariologia di S.B. da Siena,* in *Micellanea Francescana,* Vol. 47, (Roma, 1947).

[19] For the works of Cardinal de Bérulle, cf. *Oeuvres Complètes,* édition Migne, (Paris, 1856); for Olier, cf. J. J. Olier, *Oeuvres Complètes,* édition Migne, (Paris, 1856). The best texts of these two authors and also those of Gibieuf can be found in A. Molien, *La Vierge Mère de Dieu, Les meilleurs textes de l'École Française, de Bérulle-Gibieuf-Olier,* (Paris, 1940).

[20] Cf. J. B. Crasset, S.J., *La véritable Dévotion envers la Sainte Vierge Établie et Défendue,* (Paris, 1679).

[21] Cf. L. F. D'Argentan, O.F.M. Cap., *Conférences Théologiques et Spirituelles sur les grandeurs de la Très Sainte Vierge Marie, Mère de Dieu,* (Paris, 1687).

[22] Cf. F. Poiré, S.J., *La Triple Couronne de la Bienheureuse Vierge Mère de Dieu,* (Paris, 1639).

[23] "J'avais en vue ... d'aller me former aux missions et particulièrement à faire le catéchisme aux pauvre gens ... je sens de grands désirs de faire aimer Notre Seigneur et sa sainte Mère et d'aller d'une manière pauvre et simple, faire le catéchisme aux pauvres de la campagne" (*Lettres,* pp. 77 ff.)

[24] "Je parle particulièrement aux pauvres et aux simples, qui étant de bonne volonté et ayant plus de foi que le commun des savants, croient plus simplement et avec plus de mérite, je me contente de leur déclarer simplement la verité" (*V.Dév.,* no. 26).

[25] Cf. *ibid,* no. 110.

[26] For the testimonies of Popes, Bishops and theologians regarding the value of St. Louis' writings, cf. G. Ghidotti, S.M.M., *Influence mariale de Montfort, Concert des Théologiens,* in *Marie,* Vol.

VI, Septembre-Octobre (1952), pp. 62 ff; D. Huot, S.M.M., *L'Influence Mariale de Saint Louis-Marie de Montfort, Témoignages de l'Épiscopat,* in *ibid.,* p. 98 ff.

[27] Cf. *Le Traité de la Vraie Dévotion à la Très Sainte Vierge* (Louvain, 1947). English translation: *True Devotion to the Blessed Virgin Mary,* (Bay Shore, 1975).

[28] Cf. *Le Secret de Marie* (Lyon, 1926). English translation: *The Secret of Mary,* (Bay Shore, 1975).

[29] Cf. *Le Secret Admirable du Très Saint Rosaire pour se Convertir et se Sauver,* (Paris, 1912). English translation: *The Secret of the Rosary* (Bay Shore, 1974).

[30] Cf. *L'Amour de la Sagesse Eternelle,* (Pontchâteau, 1929). English translation: *The Love of the Eternal Wisdom* (Bay Shore, 1960).

[31] Cf. *Lettre Circulaire aux Amis de la Croix,* (Tourcoing, 1947). English translation: *A Circular Letter to the Friends of the Cross* (Bay Shore, 1972).

[32] Cf. *Pour Bien Mourir* (Saint Laurent-sur-Sèvre, 1927). English translation: *Preparation for a Happy Death* (Bay Shore, 1954).

[33] Cf. *Prière pour demander des Missionnaires de la Compagnie de Marie,* in edition 'Secret,' op.cit., pp. 80-96. English translation: *Prayer For Missionaries* (Bay Shore, 1954).

[34] Cf. *Allocution Aux Associés de la Compagnie de Marie,* edition *Secret, op. cit.,* pp. 97-104. No English publication.

[35] Cf. *Règle des Filles de la Sagesse* (Poitiers, 1818). No English publication.

[36] Cf. *Règle de la Compagnie de Marie,* in *Vade Mecum du Montfortain,* (Tours, 1932). No English publication.

[37] Excerpts from the *Cahier de Notes* have been published in *Saint Louis-Marie Grignion de Montfort, Oeuvres Complètes* (Paris, 1966), pp. 1695 ff. The manuscript is found at the Generalate of the Montfort Missionaries, Rome.

[38] Excerpts from the *Cahier de Sermons* have been published in the *Oeuvres Complètes* mentioned above, pp. 1707 ff. The manuscript is found at the Generalate of the Montfort Missionaries, Rome.

[39] Cf. *Lettres du Bx. Louis-Marie de Montfort* (St. Laurent-sur-Sevre, 1928): No English publication.

[40] Cf. *Cantiques du Bienheureux de Montfort* (Pontchateau, 1929). No English publication.

[41] As noted above, the excellent critical edition of Montfort's works, *Oeuvres complètes de saint Louis-Marie Grignion de Montfort* (Paris, 1966) omits some of Montfort's *Cantiques* and also sections of both the *Cahier de Sermons (Sermon Notebook)* and the *Cahier*

de Notes (*Notebook*). However, it does include some few pages of Saint Louis not listed in the bibliograhpy most of which are found only in his early biographers, e.g. *Rule for the White Penitents*. These pages have also been included in this study.

[42] R. Panikkar, *Dimensioni mariane della vita*, (Vicenza, 1972), quoted in E. Carroll, *A Survey of Recent Mariology*, in *Marian Studies*, Vol. XXV (1974), p. 106.

[43] Cf. *AAS*, Vol. 39 (1947), p. 331.

[44] His Holiness, Paul VI, Apostolic Exhortation, *Marialis Cultus*, U.S. Catholic Conference (Washington, 1974), p. 3.

PART ONE

[1] Cf. A. Josselin, S.M.M., St. Louis-Marie de Montfort, Maître de Spiritualité, in *Marie*, Nicolet, Vol. VI, Septembre-Octobre (1952), p. 8.

[2] A. Widenfeld, *Monita Salutaria B.V.M. ad Cultores Suos Indiscretos* (Gandavi, 1673). This book was condemned by Rome in 1674. For an interesting and perhaps too indulgent study of this pamphlet, cf. P. Hoffer, *La dévotion a Marie au déclin du XVIIIᵉ siècle, autour du Jansénisme et des "Avis Salutaires de la B.V.M. à ses Dévots Indiscrets*," (Paris, 1938). For an excellent study of Montfort's Marian devotion in the context of Widenfeld's work, cf. S. DeFiores, S.M.M., *La devozione mariana del Montfort nel contexto della polemica degli 'Avvisi salutari' di Widenfeld*, in *Marianum*, 36 (1974), 40-69.

[3] "Nullus Bernardo similior," from the epitaph inscribed on St. Louis de Montfort's tomb in the parish church of St. Laurent-sur-Sevre, Vendée, France.

[4] Cf. *S.Th.* II-II, q. 82, a. 1.

[5] Blain, J. B., *Abrégé de la vie de Louis-Marie Grignion de Montfort. Texte établi, présenté et annoté par Louis Pérouas*, Centre International Montfortain (Roma, 1973). Cf. S. DeFiores, S.M.M., *Itinerario spirituale di S. Luigi Maria di Montfort (1673-1716) nel periodo fino al sacerdozio (5 giugno 1700)*, Marian Library Studies, Vol. VI (Dayton, Ohio, 1974).

[6] "Cette dévotion si sensible n'était pas en lui passagère, comme en tant d'autres enfants; elle était journalière" (J. Blain, *op. cit.*, p. 10).

[7] "Tout le monde sait qu'il ne l'appelait que sa Mère, sa bonne Mère, sa chère Mère" (*ibid.*, p. 11).

[8] Cf. *S.Th.* I, q. 13, a. 1.

[9] "Dès sa plus tendre jeunesse, il allait à elle, avec une simplicité enfantine, lui demander tous ses besoins temporels, aussi bien que

spirituels; et qu'il se tenait si assuré par la grande confiance qu'il avait en ses bontés de les obtenir, que jamais ni doutes, ni inquiétudes, ni perplexité ne l'embarrassaient sur rien. Tout, à son avis, était fait, quand il avait prié sa bonne Mère" (J. Blain, *op. cit.*, p. 11).

[10] We will cite the entire letter: "Dites à mon frère Joseph que je le prie de bien étudier, et qu'il fera un des mieux de sa classe; que pour cela, il doit mettre son étude entre les mains de sa bonne Mère, la très sainte Vierge; qu'il continue à lui rendre ses petits devoirs, elle saura bien lui donner ce qui lui est nécessaire. Je recommande la même chose à mes soeurs." (*Lettres*, p. 46).

[11] L. Le Crom, S.M.M., *Saint Louis-Marie Grignion de Montfort (1673-1716)* (Tourcoing, 1946), p. 27; cf. Blain, *op. cit.*, pp. 51-52.

[12] "detachés de tout, sans père, sans mère, sans frères, sans soeurs, sans parents selon la chair, sans amis selon le monde" (*Prière pour Missionnaires*, p. 85).

[13] "Le Seigneur est mon bon Père, Jésus est mon cher Sauveur, Marie est ma bonne Mère; Puis-je avoir plus de bonheur" (*Cantiques*, p. 495).

[14] *Lettres*, p. 48.

[15] Cf. *V.Dev.*, no. 30.

[16] This fact is brought out by an anecdote related of him at this time. Fearing that Montfort's practice of carrying a little statue of Our Lady in his pocket was mere sentimentality, his spiritual director took it from him; Saint Louis responded: "On peut m'arracher des mains l'image de ma bonne mère, mais on ne pourra jamais me l'arracher du coeur." (cf. Le Crom, S.M.M., *op.cit.*, p. 52).

[17] Cf. A. Lhoumeau, S.M.M., *La vie Spirituelle à l'Ecole de S. Louis-Marie Grignion de Montfort*, (Bruges, 1954), pp. 96 ff.

[18] Cf. *Lettres*, p. 6; L. Le Crom, S.M.M., *op. cit.*, pp. 61-62.

[19] As has been previously stated, this *Cahier* has never been published, although mimeographed copies were done in 1956 with an historical introduction by P. Eyckeler, S.M.M.

[20] There are notes from at least twenty authors. Many of these works contain quotes from the Fathers, which Saint Louis also noted.

[21] References to the spiritual maternity are to be found on the following pages of the manuscript: 7, 9, 17, 40, 54, 73, 75, 79, 85, 90, 91, 92, 93, 94, 95, 96, 98, 101, 107, 110, 111, 113, 115, 126, 127, 131, 138, 145, 154, 162, 175, 176, 180, 183, 184, 291, 292, 293, 294b, 297b, 298b, 300a.

[22] Cf. L. Le Crom, S.M.M., *op. cit.*, p. 78.

[23] "Maria es Madre nuestra, es el 'misterio de gracia' que Luis M. Grignion de Montfort se creyo llamado a evangelizar" (A. Ri-

verà, in *La Maternidad espiritual de María en San Lucas I, 26-38 y en el Apocalipsis XII*, in *Estudios Marianos*, Vol. VII (1948), p. 51).

24 *Cahier de Sermons*, p. 263.

25 Cf. L. Le Crom, S.M.M., *op. cit.*, pp. 301, 333.

26 Cf. *Lettres*, pp. 24, 33, 36, 46, 54, 62.

27 Cf. *Lettres*, p. 54.

28 Cf. M. Grandet, *La vie de Messire Louis-Marie Grignion de Montfort, prêtre du clergé* (Nantes 1724), pp. 87 ff.

29 *Ibid.*, pp. 198-199.

30 Cf. L. Le Crom, S.M.M., *op. cit.*, p. 367.

31 "donnez-moi un vrai coeur de fils pour l'honorer" (*Pour bien mourir*, p. 23).

32 "D'une confiance et d'une tendresse pour la Sainte Vierge qui n'a guère d'exemples" (J. Blain, *op. cit.*, p. 199).

33 Cf. A. Lhoumeau, *op. cit.*, p. 274.

34 "Jésus-Christ est l'alpha et l'oméga, le commencement et la fin de toutes choses" (*V.Dév.*, no. 61).

35 "Savoir Jésus-Christ, la Sagesse Incarnée, c'est assez savoir. Savoir tout et ne le pas savoir, c'est ne rien savoir" (*Sagesse*, no. 11).

36 "De quoi nous serviront toutes les autres sciences nécessaires au salut si nous ne savons celle de Jésus-Christ, qui est l'unique nécessaire et le centre où toutes doivent aboutir" (*ibid.* no. 12).

37 "Jésus-Christ, notre Sauveur, vrai Dieu et vrai homme, doit être la fin dernière de toutes nos autres dévotions; autrement elles seraient fausses et trompeuses" (*V.Dév.*, no. 61).

38 Pope Paul VI, *op. cit.*, no. 25, pp. 17-18; cf. *Behold Your Mother, Woman of Faith. A Pastoral Letter on the Blessed Virgin Mary*, U.S. Catholic Conference (Washington, 1973) nos. 6, 82.

39 *Sagesse*, no. 8; Pope Paul VI in *Marialis Cultus*, twice calls Our Lady the "Seat of Wisdom" (cf. nos. 5, 30); He also calls Jesus "Wisdom," once quoting Pope Pius IX (no. 25) and also in no. 30; for references to "Wisdom" in the Second Vatican Council, and also to articles on Our Lady, Seat of Wisdom, cf. H. du Manoir, *Liminaire*, in *Maria, Etudes sur la Sainte Vierge*, ed. H. du Manoir, Vol. VIII, (Paris, 1971), p. 22, notes 53, 55.

40 Cf. R. P. Poupon, *Le Poème de la Parfaite Consécration à Marie*, (Lyon 1947), p. 25: "Son chef Bérulle en fait un usage courant; mais il était reservé à son modeste disciple, Montfort, d'accueillir le précieux héritage, de l'exploiter d'une façon originale au point de centrer toute sa spiritualité sur cette idée de Sagesse." It is also to be noted that Montfort's famous consecration is, contrary to popular belief, not directed to Our Lady, but to the Eternal and Incarnate

Wisdom, by means of Mary. Cf. *Sagesse*, no. 223.

[41] Cf. *Sagesse*, no. 70.

[42] *Ibid.*, no. 64. Cf. M. Quéméneur, S.M.M., *La maternité de grâce chez les spirituels français du XVIIe siècle de François de Sales a Grignion de Montfort*, in *BEM*, vol. 17 (1960), p. 112. Basing himself on the Wisdom literature of the Old Testament, Montfort speaks at length on the goodness and 'approachability' of Jesus, the Incarnate Wisdom (cf. *Sagesse* no. 117-132). This must be kept in mind when we read in e.g. *The True Devotion*, of the 'fear' we should have for His Majesty and His Sanctity (cf. *V.Dev.*, no. 85).

[43] Cf. *Sagesse*, no. 203.

[44] *S.Th.* I-II, q. 113, a. 6, corp: "In quolibet autem motu quo aliquid ab altero movetur, tria requiruntur: primo, quidem, motio ipsius moventis; secundo, motus mobilis; et tertio, consummatio motus, sive perventio ad finem."

[45] Cf. *Sagesse*, passim; *Cantiques*, pp. 105-143; *V.Dév.*, nos. 61-67.

[46] Cf. *Sagesse*, nos. 181-222.

[47] *S.Th.* I-II, q. 113, a. 5, corp.: "Recessio autem et accessus in motus liberii arbitrii accipitur secundum destationem et desiderium."

[48] *Sagesse*, nos. 181-183.

[49] "Il faut que ce désir de la Sagesse soit saint et sincère en gardant fidèlement les commandements de Dieu" (*ibid.*, no. 182).

[50] *Sagesse*, nos. 184-193.

[51] *S.Th.* II-II, q. 83, a. 1, ad 1.

[52] *Sagesse*, no. 188.

[53] Prayer is treated by Montfort e.g., in his *Sagesse*, at length in his *Cantiques*, pp. 421-431 and in his too little known commentary on the Creed, Pater and Ave in *Le Secret du Rosaire*, pp. 44-78.

[54] *V. Dév.*, no. 227.

[55] *Sagesse*, no. 194-202.

[56] Cf. B. Merkelbach, *Summa theologiae moralis, Vol. III* (Desclée, 1954), p. 347; cf. K. Rahner, *Penance*, in *Encyclopedia of Theology, The Concise Sacramentum Mundi* (New York, 1975), p. 1188.

[57] Cf. *Lettre aux amis de la croix*, no. 62: "Si vous êtes vraiment amis de la croix, l'amour, qui est toujours industrieux, vous fera trouver ainsi mille petites croix dont vous vous enrichirez insensiblement."

[58] Mortification is explained by Saint Louis not only in his *Sagesse* but also in his *Lettre aux amis de la croix* (passim); in his *Cantiques* (cf. pp. 520-522) and also in his *V.Dév.* (nos. 78-82).

[59] "Voici enfin le plus grand des moyens et le plus merveilleux de tous les secrets, pour acquérir et conserver la divine Sagesse, savoir, une tendre et véritable dévotion à la Sainte Vierge" (*Sagesse*, no. 203).

[60] "Et il n'y a encore qu'elle qui par l'opération du Saint-Esprit, ait le pouvoir de l'incarner, pour ainsi dire, dans les prédestinés" (*ibid.*, 1. c.).

[61] "pour former un homme-Dieu par grace" (*Secret*, no. 17).

[62] Cf. *V.Dév.*, nos. 14, 15, 39.

[63] "nous engendre en Jésus-Christ et Jésus-Christ en nous" (*Sagesse*, no. 214).

[64] It is interesting to make the comparison between the steps St. Thomas explains in the act of justification (a motion from the state of sin to the state of grace, cf. *S.Th.* I-II, q. 113) and the steps given by Montfort in the act of union with the Divine Wisdom (a motion from worldliness to intimate union with Divine Wisdom, cf. *Sagesse*, nos. 181-222):

I

St. Thomas	MOTIO MOVENTIS	St. Louis
grace		gratia materna

II

	MOTUS MOBILIS	
detestation of sin, desire, supposing faith	Recessus a term. a quo Accessus ad term. ad quem	Universal mortification, desire, supposing knowledge of J.C. and expressed in prayer

III

Union with God forgiveness of sin	CONSUMMATIO MOTUS	Union with the Eternal and Incarnate Wisdom

[65] The first reaction of the Promoter of the Faith to the newly found *Treatise on the True Devotion to the Blessed Virgin Mary* (an unfortunate title given to the manuscript by the first publishers) was a stinging condemnation: "The devotion which the pious author proposes and upholds ... could never be approved by the Church; ... every sign of approbation or commendation of this writing must be avoided by all means." (*Positio super scriptis beatificationis and canonizationis Ven.Servi Ludovici Mariae Grignon de Montfort* [Romae, 1851] p. 23). Other censors appointed by

Rome clearly answered all objections and the book was, in 1853, officially declared to be free from all error and in no way an impediment to Montfort's beatification and canonization (cf. *ibid,* [Romae, 1853] p. 30). Hilda Graef in "Mary: A History of Doctrine and Devotion" Vol. II (New York, 1965), seems to be oblivious of the precise historical and literary context—and the personality of the author—when she so strongly criticizes Montfort's Marian doctrine, erroneously declaring that the basis of Saint Louis' devotion to Mary is because it is more humble to approach God with a mediator (cf. *V.Dév.,* n. 83). H. Graef, *op. cit.,* p. 57). H. Graef apparently wrote her criticism without reading all the works of Saint Louis and without attempting to understand the basic spirituality of Montfort. Without following the difficult rules of hermeneutics, the misunderstanding shown by H. Graef is inevitable.

[66] Cf. R. Garrigou-Lagrange, O.P., *I cento anni di un grande libro,* in *Osservatore Romano,* April 22, 1942, p. 1, where the spiritual maternity is called "una sola idea-madre" of the *True Devotion;* F. Setzer, S.M.M., *The Spiritual Maternity and Saint Louis Mary de Montfort,* in *Marian Studies,* Vol. III (1952), p. 200: The place of Mary in regard to us is conceived by Montfort as principally one of spiritual motherhood"; V. Devy, S.M.M., *La Royauté Universelle de Marie,* in *La Nouvelle Revue Mariale,* Vol. VIII (1956), p. 23: "Saint Louis-Marie de Montfort n'a pas basé son esclavage d'amour formellement sur la royauté, mais sur la maternité spirituelle de la Sainte Vierge"; J. Ghidotti, S.M.M., in his resumé of the section of the Montfort Missionaries at the 1950 Rome Mariological Congress, in *Marianum,* Vol. XIII (1951), p. 96: "Procul dubio-et omnes uno ore affirmant-Maternitas Spiritualis in Mariologia Montfortana principem locum tenet."

[67] "Avant de partir, Notre aimable frère, Daignez nous bénir avec votre mère" (*Cantiques,* p. 32).

[68] "O miracle étonnant! Dieu devient notre frère" (*ibid.* p. 40).

[69] "Elle est bonne, elle est tendre; il n'y a en elle rien d'austère ni rebutant, rien de trop sublime et de trop brillant ... elle est si charitable qu'elle ne rebute personne de ceux qui demandent son intercession, quelque pécheurs qu'ils soient" (*V.Dév.,* no. 85).

[70] *Ibid.,* no. 105.

[71] Cf. *V.Dév.,* no. 84.

[72] *Cantiques,* p. 158.

[73] *V.Dév.,* no. 144.

[74] *Ibid.,* no. 201.

[75] *Ibid.,* no. 188.

[76] *Ibid.,* no. 201.

[77] *Cantiques,* p. 165.

[78] *Cantiques*, p. 175.

[79] *Secret*, no. 8.

[80] Cf. *Oraison à Marie*, in *Secret*, p. 65.

[81] *V. Dév.*, no. 268.

[82] *Secret*, no. 22.

[83] *Ibid.*, no. 215.

[84] *Cantiques*, p. 139.

[85] *Sagesse*, no. 213.

[86] "Il n'y a jamais eu que Marie… qui ait eu le pouvoir d'incarner et mettre au monde la Sagesse Eternelle—et il n'y a encore qu'elle qui par l'opération du Saint Esprit, ait le pouvoir de l'incarner, pour ainsi dire, dans les prédestinés" (*ibid.*, no. 203).

[87] "Vous nous donnez la vie à tous en nous donnant le fruit de vie" (*Cantiques*, p. 30).

[88] "Chretiéns, apprêtez vos oreilles, écoutez-moi, prédestinés, car je raconte les merveilles de celle dont vous êtes nés" (*ibid.*, p. 166).

[89] "C'est elle qui les engendre, les porte dans son sein et les met au monde de la gloire" (*Sagesse*, no. 213).

[90] "Mon sein vous donne le jour" and as Montfort continues: "C'est moi qui vous engendre" (*Cantiques*, p. 172).

[91] *V.Dév.*, no. 258.

[92] *Ibid.*, no. 203.

[93] "Comme un enfant à la mamelle, Je suis attaché sur son sein, Cette Vierge pure et fidèle, M'y nourrit d'un lait tout divin" (*Cantiques*, p. 167).

[94] "La très sainte Vierge et ses enfants et serviteurs" (*V.Dév.* no. 183).

[95] *Ibid.*, no. 112.

[96] "enfermé dans le sein de Marie" (*Secret*, no. 14).

[97] *V.Dév.*, no. 201.

[98] *Sagesse*, no. 214; cf. Gal. 4:19.

PART TWO

[1] Cf. *S.Th.* I, *q.* 1, a, 2, corp.: "Respondeo dicendum sacram doctrinam esse scientiam." The definition of science is given by E. Hugon, *Tractatus Dogmatici*, Vol. I, (Parisiis, 1927), p. 10: "(scientia) sumitur… pro cognitione certa et evidenti conclusionum ex principiis certis, per demonstrationem quae causam ostendat, deductarum."

[2] Cf. P. Poupon, *op. cit.*, p. 609: The Trinitarian aspect of Marian devotion is underlined by Pope Paul VI *op. cit.*, no. 25.

[3] Cf. H. Denziger and A. Schönmetzer, *Enchiridion Symbolorum,*

Definitionum et Declarationum de Rebus Fidei et Morum (33rd ed., 1965), 3326.

4 Cf. K. Rahner, *Trinity, Divine*, in *Encyclopedia of Theology, The Concise Sacramentum Mundi*, (New York 1975), p. 1758.

5 Cf. M. Schmaus, *Holy Spirit*, in *ibid.*, p. 647.

6 The most thorough work on this question is C. Dillenschneider, *Le Principe Premier d'une Théologie Mariale Organique*, (Paris, 1955).

7 "a quo aliquid procedit quocumque modo" (*S.Th.* I q. 33, a. 1).

8 Cf. A. Bonnichon, *Pratique de L'Enseignement de la Théologie Mariale*, in *BEM*, Vol. II (1936), pp. 60 ff.

9 Cf. P. Bonnefoy, O.F.M., *La Primauté Absolue de Notre Seigneur Jésus-Christ et de la Très-Sainte Vierge*, in *BEM*, Vol. IV (1938) pp. 88 ff.

10 Cf. C. Dillenschneider, *op. cit.*, p. 20: "Ceux qui optent pour la perspective christique établissent comme principe d'unification de la Mariologie, l'association sotériologique de Marie, Mère de Dieu, avec son Fils Rédempteur. Ceux qui se confinent dans la perspective ecclésiale proposent... Marie, prototype de l'Eglise, soit de l'humanité rachetée"; cf. O. Semmelroth, *Dogmatic Constitution on the Church, Chapter VIII, The Role of the Blessed Virgin Mary, Mother of God, in the Mystery of Christ and the Church*, in *Commentary on the Documents of Vatican II*, ed. H. Vorgrimler, Vol. I, (New York, 1967), p. 286.

11 Montfort had not only read the opinions of many authors in the books of Mariology he consulted, but also marked in his notebook a quote from Suarez: "In ipsamet dignitate matris tamquam in radice et fonte omnia continentur" (*Cahier de Notes*, p. 184). Cf. Suarez, *Opera Omnia*, (Paris, 1866), Tom. XIX, Quaestio 36, Disput. 19.

12 Cf. *V. Dév.*, no. 243.

13 "ce mystère est un abrégé de tous les mystères, qui renferme la volonté et la grâce de tous" (*ibid.*, no. 248); cf. de Bérulle, *Oeuvres complètes, op. cit.*, col. 228.

14 "... du mystère de Jésus vivant et regnant en Marie, ou de l'Incarnation du Verbe" (*V. Dév.*, no. 248).

15 *Ibid.*, no. 243.

16 "C'est la Mère de Jésus, on n'en peut pas dire plus. Voilà la gloire des gloires, la victoire des victoires, la couronne des couronnes, que tous les mortels entonnent: au ciel, en terre, en tous lieux: Marie est Mère de Dieu. C'est la Mère de Jésus, on n'en peut pas dire plus" (*Cantiques*, p. 319).

17 Cf. *Sagesse*, no. 105-106.

18 Cf. Montfort's clear statement on the Immaculate Conception,

Cantiques, p. 163, with references of the preceding note.

[19] Cf. *V.Dév.*, no. 37; also T. Graham, S.M.M., *The Queenship of Mary*, in *Alma Socia Christi*, Vol. VIII, (Rome, 1953), p. 143.

[20] Cf. J. Hermans, S.M.M., *Maria's Middelaarschap volgens de Leer van de Heilige Louis Marie Grignion de Montfort*, (Eindhoven, 1947), p. 72 ff.; *V.Dév.*, no. 16, 22.

[21] "... son plus grand bonheur, et qui est la source de toutes les autres faveurs dont le Ciel l'a comblée, est la Maternité Divine." (H. Boudon, *Le saint esclavage de l'admirable Mère de Dieu*, [Paris, MDCCLXIX], p. 171).

[22] "Ce principe est la véritable source de toutes les grandeurs de la Sainte Vierge" (L. D'Argentan, *op. cit.*, Vol. I, p. 455).

[23] "Sa maternité divine est le fondement de toutes ses grandeurs" (J. Crasset, *op. cit.*, Vol. II, p. 14).

[24] "Le premier est celui de Mère de Dieu ... où toutes ses grandeurs ... prennent leur origine" (F. Poiré, *op. cit.*, Vol. I, p. 365). For the thought of the French School of spirituality on this point, cf. A. Molien, *op. cit.*, p. 32.

[25] "Dieu racheta le monde par l'Ave Maria" (*Cantiques*, p. 135).

[26] Cf. *V.Dév.*, no. 74: "Jésus-Christ, l'ayant choisie pour la compagne indissoluble de sa vie, de sa mort, de sa gloire et de sa puissance au ciel et sur la terre." (cf. *ibid.*, no. 37; *Cantiques*, p. 154).

[27] Saint Louis also makes use of the secondary principles of Mariology:

    a) *Principium convenientiae*: "Je m'étonne qu'on en raisonne, Dieu l'a bien pu, je soutiens qu'il l'a dû" (*Cantiques*, p. 163). Montfort uses this principle when speaking about the Immaculate Conception (*ibid.*, 1. c.).

    b) *Principium analogiae*: "Ce que je dis absolument de Jésus-Christ, je le dis relativement de la Sainte Vierge" (*V.Dév.*, no. 74).

    c) *Principium eminentiae*: "Elle surpasse tout ce qui n'est pas Dieu" (*Cantiques*, p. 161); "pourvu qu'on la mette au dessous de Dieu, on n'en peut assez dire" (*Cahier de Sermons*, p. 147).

[28] Cf. Pope Paul, *op. cit.*, nos. 15, 30.

[29] Cf. *Dogmatic Constitution on the Church*, in *Documents of Vatican II*, (New York, 1966), e.g., nos. 53, 56, 61, 62.

[30] Cf. *op. cit.*, e.g. nos. 18, 71, 117.

[31] "Dieu le Père se veut faire des enfants par Marie" (*V.Dév.*, no. 29).

[32] "Demeurez en Jacob, c'est-à-dire, faites votre demeure et résidence dans mes enfants et prédestinés, figurés par Jacob et non point dans les enfants du diable et les réprouvés, figurés par Esau" (*ibid.*, 1. c.).

[33] "C'est à Marie que Dieu le Père a dit: *In Jacob inhabità*: Ma fille, demeurez en Jacob, c'est-à-dire, dans les prédestinés figurés par Jacob" (*Secret*, no. 15).

[34] Cf. A. Plessis, S.M.M., *Commentaire du Traité de la vraie dévotion à la sainte Vierge du Bx. Grignion de Montfort*, (Pontchateau, 1943), p. 103. It is interesting to see how Scriptural scholarship has developed. In 1936, H. Gebhard, S.M.M., could declare that the majority of scholars see in Jacob and Esau the figure of the elect and the damned, and this apparently in a true scriptural sense. (cf. Revue des prêtres de Marie, Février, 1936, p. 45).

[35] Cf. *Sagesse*, no. 23.

[36] "pour lui donner le pouvoir de produire son Fils et tous les membres de son corps mystique" (*V.Dév.*, no. 17).

[37] "La conduite que les trois Personnes de la sainte Trinité ont tenue dans l'Incarnation et le premier avènement de Jésus-Christ, elles la gardent tous les jours, d'une manière invisible, dans la Sainte Église, et la garderont jusqu'à la consommation des siècles, dans le dernier avènement de Jésus-Christ" (*ibid.*, no. 22).

[38] *Ibid.*, no. 29.

[39] "Dieu, ayant voulu commencer et achever ses plus grands ouvrages par la très sainte Vierge depuis qu'il l'a formée, il est à croire qu'il ne changera point de conduite dans les siècles des siècles car il est Dieu et ne change point en ses sentiments ni en sa conduite" (*ibid.*, no. 15).

[40] "Dieu le Père n'a donné son Unique au monde que par Marie" (*ibid.*, no. 16).

[41] "Il l'a donné à Marie afin que le monde le reçût par elle" (*ibid.*, 1. c.).

[42] Cf. *Cantiques*, p. 135.

[43] Cf. *V.Dév.*, no. 248.

[44] Cf. *op. cit.*, no. 69; *ibid.*, nos. 78, 83.

[45] The French and English text of this agreement can be found in a review called *Orthodoxy of the Catholic Doctrine*, Vol. 4, no. 3 (July-September 1975), p. 11.

[46] Mary's fulness of grace is more often, in the doctrine of Saint Louis, attributed to God the Father (cf. *V.Dév.*, no. 23) although it is at times attributed also to the Son (cf. *Cantiques*, p. 113) and the Holy Spirit (cf. *V.Dév.*, no. 25).

[47] Cf. M. Llamera, O.P., *La maternidad espiritual de María*, in *Estudios Marianos*, Vol. III (1944), p. 110 ff.; Gregorio de Jesus Crucificado, O.C.D., *Naturaleza de la Maternidad espiritual*, in *Estudios Marianos*, Vol. VII (1948), pp. 138 ff.

[48] Cf. G. Garces, C.M.F., *Mater Corredemptrix*, (Romae MCMXL), pp. 267 ff.

[49] "Dieu le Fils a communiqué à sa Mère tout ce qu'il a acquis par sa vie et par sa mort, ses mérites infinis et ses vertus admirables, et il l'a faite la trésorière de tout ce que son Père lui a donné en héritage; c'est par elle qu'il applique ses mérites à ses membres, qu'il communique ses vertus et distribue ses grâces; c'est son canal mystérieux, c'est son aqueduc, par où il fait passer doucement et abondamment ses miséricordes" (*V.Dév.*, no. 24).

[50] "Cette bonne mère... nous revêt des habits propres, neufs, précieux et parfumés d'Esau l'aîné, c'est-à-dire, de Jésus-Christ son Fils, qu'elle garde dans sa maison, c'est-à-dire qu'elle a dans sa puissance, étant la trésorière et la dispensatrice universelle des mérites et des vertus de son Fils, Jésus-Christ, qu'elle donne et communique à qui elle veut et autant qu'elle veut" (*ibid.*, no. 206).

[51] "Elle est... l'océan immense de toutes les grandeurs de Dieu, le grand magasin de tous ses biens, le trésor inepuisable du Seigneur et la trésorière et la dispensatrice de tous ses dons... Il ne descend aucun don céleste sur la terre qu'il ne passe par elle comme par un canal. C'est de sa plénitude que nous avons tous reçu..." (*Sagesse*, no. 207). Cf. *Secret*, no. 9.

[52] *Secret*, no. 17.

[53] "Quiconque donc, veut être membre de Jésus-Christ, plein de grace et de vérité, doit être formé en Marie par le moyen de la grâce de Jésus-Christ qui réside en elle en plénitude, pour être communiquée en plénitude aux vrais membres de Jésus-Christ et à ses vrais enfants" (*Secret*, no. 12).

[54] "(Elle) se donne aussi tout entière et d'une manière ineffable à celui qui lui donne tout. Elle le fait s'engloutir dans l'abîme de ses grâces; elle l'orne de ses mérites" (*V.Dév.*, no. 144).

[55] "dans ce sein virginal, l'âme y soit nourrie du lait de sa grâce et de sa miséricorde maternelle" (*ibid.*, no. 264).

[56] Cf. *Cantiques*, p. 144.

[57] Cf. *Cantiques*, p. 147.

[58] "Elle donne un nouveau parfum et une nouvelle grâce à ces habits et ornements en leur communiquant ses propres habits: ses mérites et ses vertus... en sorte que tous ses domestiques, ses fidèles serviteurs et esclaves sont doublement vêtu, des habits de son Fils et des siens propres" (*V.Dév.*, no. 30).

[59] Pope Paul VI, *op. cit.*, no. 57.

[60] "Comme dans l'ordre naturel, il faut qu'un enfant ait un père et une mère, de même dans la génération surnaturelle et spirituelle il y a un père qui est Dieu et une mère qui est Marie" (*V.Dév.*, no. 30).

[61] "Comme dans l'ordre naturel, il faut qu'un enfant ait un père et une mère, de même dans l'ordre de la grâce, il faut qu'un vrai

enfant de l'Église ait Dieu pour père et Marie pour Mère" (*Secret*, no. 11).

⁶² That this is a mere comparison is seen not only by the nature of the statement, but also by the fact that F. Poiré (*op. cit.*, Vol. IV, p. 30) who is most probably the source of this declaration of Montfort, declares: "c'était une chose très convenable que pour être de tout point accomplie," (Poiré has just declared that predestination is a type of generation), "il y eut un Père et une Mère."

⁶³ "qui n'a pas Marie pour Mère n'a pas Dieu pour Père ... Hélas, Dieu le Père n'a pas dit à Marie de faire sa demeure en eux, parce qu'ils sont des Ésaus" (*V.Dév.*, no. 30).

⁶⁴ "Dieu le Saint-Esprit veut se former en elle et par elle des élus" (*V.Dév.*, no. 34).

⁶⁵ "*In electis meis mitte radices.* Jetez, ma bien aimée et mon Épouse, les racines de toutes vos vertus dans mes élus" (*ibid.*, no. 34).

⁶⁶ "C'est à Marie que Dieu le Saint-Esprit a dit: "*In electis meis mitte radices*: Jetez, ma fidele épouse, des racines en mes élus" (*Secret*, no. 15).

⁶⁷ *V.Dév.*, no. 34.

⁶⁸ *Ibid.*, no. 6.

⁶⁹ "La hauteur de ses mérites ... ne se peut apercevoir ... la largeur de sa charité ... ne se peut mesurer ... la grandeur de sa puissance ... ne se peut comprendre ... la profondeur de son humilité et de toutes ses vertus et ses grâces qui sont un abîme, ne se peut sonder. O Hauteur incompréhensible! O largeur ineffable! O grandeur démesurée! O abîme impénétrable!" (*ibid.*, no. 7).

⁷⁰ Cf. *ibid.*, no. 5.

⁷¹ "J'ai pris tant de complaisance en vous lorsque vous viviez sur la terre dans la pratique des plus sublimes vertus" (*V.Dév.*, no. 34).

⁷² "Je désire encore vous trouver sur la terre, sans cesser d'être dans le ciel" (*ibid.*, 1. c.).

⁷³ "Reproduisez-vous ... dans mes élus; que je vois en eux avec complaisance les racines de votre foi invincible, de votre humilité profonde, de votre mortification universelle, de votre oraison sublime, de votre charité ardente, de votre espérance ferme et de toutes vos vertus" (*ibid.*, 1. c.).

⁷⁴ *Ibid.*, no. 206.

⁷⁵ "des copies vivantes de Marie" (*ibid.*, no. 217). Montfort wants us to become living copies of Mary "pour aimer et glorifier Jésus-Christ" (*ibid.*, l.c.). Mary is the means to reach our end, Jesus Christ.

⁷⁶ "trouvant sa chère Épouse comme reproduite dans les âmes" (*ibid.*, no. 217).

[77] "Le Saint-Esprit, ayant epousé Marie... continue a produire tous les jours en elle et par elle, d'une manière mystérieuse, mais véritable, les prédestinés" (*Secret*, no. 13).

[78] This term is found throughout the writings of Montfort. Cf. *V.Dév.*, nos. 5, 20, 25, 35, 36; *Prière pour Missionnaires*, p. 88; *Secret*, nos. 13, 15.

[79] At times Saint Louis explicitly terms this relationship a "union" (cf. *V.Dév.*, no. 35) through which Mary is the "companion of the Holy Spirit" (cf. *ibid.*, no. 37).

[80] Cf. *ibid.*, nos. 50, 64, 145, 158, *Secret*, no. 17; *Sagesse*, no. 224.

[81] "Dieu le Saint-Esprit... est devenu fécond par Marie qu'il a epousée. C'est avec elle et en elle et d'elle qu'il a produit son chef-d'oeuvre qui est un Dieu fait homme" (*V.Dév.*, no. 20).

[82] "Cet Amour substantiel du Père et du Fils a epousé Marie pour produire Jésus-Christ" (*ibid.*, no. 36).

[83] Cf. *S.Th.*, III, q. 32, a. 3 ad 1.

[84] "Quel grand mystère! L'ombre seule du Saint Esprit, En elle forma Jésus-Christ, La fit sa mère, Sans en devenir le père" (*Cantiques*, p. 177).

[85] *V. Dév.*, no. 36.

[86] *Ibid.*, no. 37.

[87] *Ibid.*, no. 36.

[88] "C'est vous seul qui formez toutes les personnes divines hors de la divinité" (*Prière pour Missionnaires*, p. 89).

[89] "Venez, Saint-Esprit, qui faites les martyrs, les confesseurs, les apôtres, les prophêtes, les grands héros, les grands coeurs" (*Cantiques*, p. 20).

[90] *V.Dév.*, no. 37.

[91] "Vous avez formé le chef des prédestinés avec elle et en elle; c'est avec elle et en elle que vous devez former tous ses membres" (*Prière pour Missionnaires*, pp. 88-89).

[92] "Ayant produit en elle et par elle et d'elle, Jésus-Christ, ce chef-d'oeuvre, le Verbe Incarné... Il continue à produire tous les jours en elle et par elle d'une manière mystérieuse... les prédestinés (*Secret*, no. 13).

[93] Cf. *V.Dév.*, no. 21.

[94] Cf. J. Pintard, *La maternité spirituelle de Marie selon les théologiens du XIXe siècle*, in *BEM*, Vol. 17, (1960), p. 140. Pintard does not appear to realize that the text under discussion by Pusey and Newman is taken from these numbers of the *True Devotion;* cf. J. Stern *Le Saint-Esprit et Marie chez Newman et Faber*, in *BEM*, Vol. 26, (1969), pp. 37-56, and his bibliography; cf. J. H. Newman *A Letter Addressed to the Rev. E. B. Pusey* in *Certain Difficulties Felt By Anglicans*, Vol. II, (London, 1885).

[95] Cf. De Rosa, *La fecondità dello Spirito Santo*, in *Marianum*, Vol. X, (1948), p. 65-72; P. Oger, *Intorno ad un passo* ... in *Marianum*, Vol. X, (1948), p. 369; J. M. Alonso, *Hacia una Mariologia Trinitaria*, in Estudios Marianos, Vol. X, (1950), p. 183 and also in *Ephemerides Mariologicae*, I, (1951), p. 351.

[96] Cf. G. Philips, *Le Saint Esprit et Marie dans l'Eglise, Vatican II et Prospective du Probleme*, in *BEM*, Vol. 25, 1968, pp. 31-32; M. Dupuy, *Le Saint-Esprit et Marie dans l'Ecole Française*, in *BEM*, Vol. 26, 1969, pp. 27-32.

[97] "Dieu le Saint-Esprit, étant stérile en Dieu, c'est-à-dire ne produisant point d'autre personne divine, est devenu fécond par Marie qu'il a épousée. C'est avec elle et en elle et d'elle qu'il produit son chef-d'oeuvre, qui est un Dieu fait homme, et qu'il produit tous les jours jusqu'à la fin du monde les prédestinés et les membres du corps de ce chef adorable: c'est pourquoi plus il trouve Marie, sa chère et indissoluble Épouse, dans une âme, et plus il devient opérant et puissant pour produire Jésus-Christ en cette âme et cette âme en Jésus-Christ. (no. 20). Cé n'est pas qu'on veuille dire que la Très Sainte Vierge donne au Saint-Esprit la fécondité, comme s'il ne l'avait pas, puisque, étant Dieu, il a la fécondité ou la capacité de produire, comme le Père et le Fils, quoiqu'il ne la réduise pas à l'acte, ne produisant point d'autre Personne divine. Mais on veut dire que le Saint-Esprit, par l'entremise de la Sainte Vierge, dont il veut bien se servir, quoiqu'il n'en ait pas absolument besoin, réduit à l'acte sa fécondité, en produisant en elle et par elle Jésus-Christ et ses membres. Mystère de grâce inconnu même aux plus savants et spirituels d'entre les chrétiens" (no. 21) cf. *ibid.*, no. 164.

[98] Cf. *Dogmatic Constitution on the Church*, in *op. cit.*, e.g. nos. 64, 65, 68.

[99] *Cahier de Notes*, p. 9.

[100] F. Poiré, *op. cit.*, Vol. I, pp. 126-127.

[101] J. Terrien, *La Mère de Dieu et la Mère des Hommes*, Vol. I, (Paris, 1900), p. 202.

[102] Poupon, *op. cit.*, p. 613.

[103] Paul VI, *op. cit.*, no. 26.

[104] Cf. E. Schillebeeckx, *The Understanding of Faith*, (New York, 1974), p. 57.

[105] Cf. d'Argentan, *op. cit.*, 1ère conférence, art. 4; *3e conférence*, art. 3, pp. 21, 312-314 (cf. *Cahier de Notes*, 163, 172); cf. de Bérulle, *Discours*, IV, 2 in Migne, 208.

[106] *V.Dév.*, no. 20.

[107] Cf. G. Philips, *art. cit.*, pp. 31-32; for another interpretation of de Bérulle, cf. M. Dupuy, *art. cit.*, pp. 27-28.

[108] G. Philips, *art. cit.*, p. 32.

[109] *V.Dév.*, no. 21.

[110] G. Philips, *art. cit.*, 1. c.

[111] Montfort often calls Mary 'divine,' not only because she, as anyone else sharing sanctifying grace, possesses divine life—and she, in an intense degree; but also because she has given birth to the God-Man, and now as Mother of men gives us this divine life of grace.

[112] "O Saint-Esprit! donnez-moi une grande dévotion et un grand penchant vers votre divine Épouse, un grand appui sur son sein maternel et un recours continuel à sa miséricorde, afin qu'en elle vous formiez en moi Jésus-Christ au naturel, grand et puissant, jusqu'à la plénitude de son âge parfait. Ainsi-soit-il." (*Prière à Jésus*, in *Secret*, p. 62).

[113] "Dieu le Fils veut se former et pour ainsi dire, s'incarner tous les jours par sa chère Mère, dans ses membres" (*V. Dév.*, no. 31).

[114] "Jamais Dieu n'a fait et formé qu'une inimitié, mais irréconciliable, qui durera et augmentera même jusques à la fin: c'est entre Marie, sa digne Mère, et le diable; entre les enfants et serviteurs de la sainte Vierge et les enfants et suppôts de Lucifer; en sorte que la plus terrible des ennemies que Dieu ait faite contre le diable est Marie, sa sainte Mère. Il lui a même donné, dès le paradis terrestre, quoiqu'elle ne fût encore que dans son idée, tant de haine contre ce maudit ennemi de Dieu..." (*V.Dév.*, no. 52).

[115] *Ibid.*, 1. c.

[116] "Non seulement Dieu a mis une inimitié mais des inimitiés, non seulement entre Marie et le démon, mais entre la race de la sainte Vierge et la race du démon: c'est-à-dire que Dieu a mis des inimitiés, des antipathies et haines secrètes entre les vrais enfants et serviteurs de la Sainte Vierge et les *enfants et esclaves du diable*" (*ibid.*, no. 54). In his *Prière pour Missionnaires* (p. 87) Montfort explicitly calls his congregation "bienheureuse postérité de Marie" when speaking about this same text.

[117] "Ils seront petits et pauvres selon le monde et abaissés devant tous comme le talon" (*V.Dév.*, no. 54); cf. *Prière pour Missionnaires*, p. 87.

[118] "en union de Marie, ils écraseront la tête du diable" (*V.Dév.*, no. 54).

[119] Cf. J. Skinner, *A Critical and Exegetical Commentary on the Book of Genesis*, (Edinburgh, 1910), p. 81. Scholars also list Gunkel, von Rad, Zimmerli to be of the same opinion.

[120] Cf. E. May, *Mary in the Old Testament*, in *Mariology*, ed. J. B. Carol, Vol. 1, (Milwaukee, 1954), pp. 56-62.

[121] C. Miller, "*As It Is Written*," *The Use of Old Testament References in the Documents of Vatican Council II*, (St. Louis, 1973),

p. 56; E. Maly, in *Genesis*, in *The Jerome Biblical Commentary*, (Englewood Cliffs, New Jersey, 1968), making no mention of Mary in his commentary on the protoevangelium, does declare: "Later revelation will confirm this first vague message of victory and specify the manner in which the victory will be attained" (no. 28).

[122] *The Dogmatic Constitution on the Church*, in *op. cit.*, no. 55.

[123] "*In Israel haereditare*... Ayez Israel pour heritage" (*V.Dév.*, no. 31).

[124] "C'est à Marie que Dieu le Fils a dit: *In Israel haereditare*: Ma chere Mère, ayez votre héritage en Israel, c'est-à-dire, dans les prédestinés" (*Secret*, no. 15).

[125] "comme leur bonne mère, vous les enfanterez, nourrirez, élèverez; et comme leur souveraine, vous les conduirez, gouvernerez et défendrez" (*V.Dév.*, no. 31).

[126] "Un homme et un homme est né en elle, dit le Saint-Esprit! *Homo et homo natus est in ea.* Selon l'explication de quelques Pères, le premier homme qui est né de Marie est l'Homme-Dieu, Jésus-Christ; le second est un homme pur, enfant de Dieu et de Marie par adoption" (*ibid.*, no. 32). The RSV translation of this text reads: "And of Zion it shall be said, 'This one and that one were born in her'; for the Most High himself will establish her."

[127] Cf. the application made by J. Olier, *Oeuvres*, Migne, col. 883.

[128] Cf. *Cahier de Notes*, p. 180.

[129] S. Bonaventura, *Speculum B.M.V.*, Lect. III, 1 20 in *Opera Omnia*, Vol. XIV, p. 238.

[130] Cf. Origen, *In Evang. S. Joan.*, *P.G.*, Vol. XII, 1547.

[131] Cf. J. Crasset, *op. cit.*, Vol. I, p. 35.

[132] "Par la salutation angélique, Dieu s'est fait homme, une Vierge est devenue Mère de Dieu, les âmes des justes ont été délivrées des limbes... les trônes vides ont été remplis, le péché a été pardonné, la grâce nous a été donnée" (*Secret du Rosaire*, p. 50).

[133] Cf. *Cantiques*, p. 135.

[134] Cf. *Secret du Rosaire*, p. 49: "La Sainte Vierge a été celle à qui cette divine salutation a été presentée pour terminer l'affaire la plus grande et la plus importante du monde, l'Incarnation... et la rédemption."

[135] Cf. A. Rivera, *La maternidad espiritual de Maria en San Lucas 1:26-38 y en el Apocalipsis XII*, in *Estudios Marianos*, Vol. VII (1948), pp. 51 ff.

[136] Cf. *V.Dév.*, nos. 179, 216; also in *Oraison à Jésus*, in *Secret*, p. 60.

[137] Cf. J. Nouet, *Retraite pour se préparer à la Mort*, (Paris, 1698), pp. 261-263.

[138] "O Jésus! qui avez témoigné en mourant la tendresse de votre

coeur envers votre Bienheureuse Mère, et qui lui avez recommandé tous vos disciples en la personne de saint Jean: mettez-moi, s'il vous plait, sous sa protection et donnez-moi un vrai coeur de fils pour l'honorer" (*Pour bien mourir*, pp. 22-23).

[139] "Souvenez-vous, ô Marie, que votre Fils sur l'Arbre de la Croix vous a recommandé mon âme: montrez-lui que vous êtes une bonne Mère et que vous prenez soin de mon salut; *Monstra te esse Matrem*" (*ibid.*, p. 23).

[140] "Souvenez-vous, Seigneur de votre congrégation...que vous avez possédée dans votre coeur, lorsque votre cher Fils, mourant sur la croix, l'arrosait de son sang et la consacrait par sa mort, en la confiant à sa sainte Mère" (*Prière pour Missionnaires*, p. 81).

[141] Cf. B. Vawter, *The Gospel According to John*, in *The Jerome Biblical Commentary*, op. cit., no. 170: "It is also, however, a 'sign' of the spiritual motherhood of Mary, the new Eve, the mother of the faithful," cf. *Behold Your Mother*, op. cit., no. 37.

[142] Montfort's omission of this proof in his works on Our Lady seems even stranger when we consider that the text "Behold Thy Mother" is explained by many authors known to Montfort and is even included in his *Cahier de Notes* (p. 131).

[143] Cf. T. Koehler, *Maternité Spirituelle de Marie*, in *Maria, Etudes sur la Sainte Vierge*, Vol. I, (Paris 1949), p. 583: "Les paroles du Christ, loin de créer la maternité de grâce, ne prennent leur sens qu'en la supposant."

[144] Saint Louis himself testifies to his study of the Fathers in no. 41 and in no. 118 of his *True Devotion;* his numerous quotations from the Fathers in his *Cahier de Notes* bear witness to this truth.

[145] Cf. *V.Dév.*, no. 26.

[146] "Remarquez que non seulement Marie est la Mère de Jésus, le chef de tous les élus—mais encore qu'elle est (la Mère) de tous ses membres...c'est la doctrine des saints Pères" (*Sagesse*, no. 213).

[147] Cf. J. Bover, *La Maternidad Espiritual de Maria en los Padres Griegos*, in *Estudios Marianos*, Vol. VII (1948), pp. 91 ff.

[148] Cf. J. Garreta, *La Maternidad Espiritual de Maria en los Padres Latinos*, in *ibid.*, pp. 105 ff.

[149] Cf. G. Joussard, *Maternité spirituelle de la Vierge, premières amorces dans la Tradition*, in *BEM*, Vol. 16 (1959), pp. 55-86.

[150] Cf. W. O'Connor, *The Spiritual Maternity of Our Lady in Tradition*, in *Marian Studies*, Vol. III (1952), pp. 142 ff.

[151] Cf. J. Terrien, op. cit., Vol. I, 2ème partie, p. 23: "Nous avions donc raison de l'affirmer, l'universalité de cette doctrine, à travers les différents âges et les differents pays, démontre avec evidence qu'elle nous vient des sources même de la révélation."

[152] Cf. S. Augustinus, *De Sancta Virginitate*, 6, *P.L.*, Vol. 40, 399.

[153] Cf. S. Leo Magnus, *Sermo 26*, *P.L.*, Vol. 54, 213.

[154] Cf. S. Ambrosius, (apocryphal) *In Apocalypsin*, *P.L.*, Vol. 17, 876.

[155] "Saint Augustin, se surpassant soi-même et tout ce que je viens de dire, dit que tous les prédestinés, pour être conformes a l'image du Fils de Dieu, sont en ce monde cachés dans le sein de la très sainte Vierge, où il sont gardés, nourris, entretenus et agrandis par cette bonne Mère, jusqu'à ce qu'elle ne les enfante à la gloire après la mort, qui est proprement le jour de leur naissance" (*V.Dév.*, no. 33).

[156] "Saint Augustin dit que les élus sont dans le sein de Marie, et qu'elle ne les met au monde que lorsqu'ils entrent dans la gloire" (*Sagesse*, no. 213).

[157] "Saint Augustin dit même que dans ce monde les prédestinés sont tous enfermés dans le sein de Marie, et qu'ils ne viennent au jour que lorsque cette bonne Mère les enfante à la vie éternelle" (*Secret*, no. 14).

[158] F. Poiré, *op. cit.*, Vol. III, p. 385. Cf. *Cahier de Notes*, p. 75.

[159] S. Augustinus, *De Sacra Virginitate*, *P.L.*, Vol. 40, 399.

[160] Cf. E. Neubert, *Marie dans le dogme*, Paris (1954), p. 95.

[161] Cf. S. Augustinus (apocryphal) *De symbolo ad catechumenos sermo alius*, *P.L.*, Vol. XL, 659 ff. The text is attributed to Quodvultdeus, Bishop of Carthage. Cf. *Dogmatic Constitution on the Church*, in *op. cit.*, no. 53.

[162] "Saint Augustin appelle la sainte Vierge *forma Dei*: le moule de Dieu: '*Si formam Dei te appellem, digna existis*'; le moule propre à former et mouler des dieux. Celui qui est jeté dans ce moule divin est bientôt formé et moulé en Jésus-Christ et Jésus-Christ en lui" (*V.Dév.*, no. 219).

[163] *Oeuvres complètes de Monsieur Tronson*, Migne, t. II, col. 577.

[164] S. Augustinus (aprocryphal) *Sermo 208*, *P.L.*, Vol. 39, 2131. This text is now attributed to Ambrose Autpert.; cf. R. Laurentin, *op. cit.*, p. 129.

[165] Montfort, although speaking of the doctrine of the New Eve (cf. *V.Dév.*, nos. 53, 175)—though never calling her by this title— insists more on Our Lady as the indissoluble companion of the Redeemer.

[166] "Vous nous donnez la vie, puisque vous brisez nos liens" (*Cantiques*, p. 40).

[167] Such doctrine is familiar to the entire French School of spirituality. Cf. Cardinal de Bérulle, in Migne, *Opusc. Divers de Piété*, XCIII, 1103; Gibeuf, *Vie et Grandeurs de la Vierge*, Tome I, Ch. 2, cited by P. Poupon, *op. cit.*, p. 595.

[168] "Jésus-Christ, l'ayant choisie pour la compagne indissoluble de sa vie, de sa mort, de sa gloire et de sa puissance au ciel et sur la terre" (V.Dév., no. 74).

[169] "Ils semblent tous deux confondus. Que l'alliance est belle! Marie est toute dans Jésus... ou pour mieux dire, elle n'est plus, mais Jésus seul en elle" (Cantiques, p. 154).

[170] "Ils sont unis si intimement que l'un est tout dans l'autre: Jésus est tout en Marie et Marie toute en Jésus; ou plutôt, elle n'est plus, mais Jesus seul en elle; et on séparerait plutôt la lumière du soleil que Marie de Jésus. En sorte qu'on peut nommer Notre-Seigneur, Jésus de Marie et la Sainte Vierge, Marie de Jésus" (V.Dév., no. 247).

[171] "Je me tourne içi un moment vers vous, ô mon aimable Jésus, pour me plaindre amoureusement à votre divine Majesté, de ce que la plupart des chrétiens même les plus savants, ne savent pas la liaison nécessaire qui est entre vous et votre sainte Mère. Vous êtes, Seigneur, toujours avec Marie et Marie est toujours avec vous et ne peut être sans vous: autrement elle cesserait d'être ce qu'elle est... Elle (vous) est si intimement unie qu'on séparerait plutôt la lumière du soleil, la chaleur du feu: je dis plus, on séparerait plutôt tous les anges et les saints de vous que la divine Marie" (V.Dév., no. 63).

[172] cf. Sagesse, nos. 204, 206; Secret, nos. 56, 78; V. Dév., nos. 33, 44, 77.

[173] Constitution on the Sacred Liturgy in op. cit., no. 103.

[174] Dogmatic Constitution on the Church, in op. cit., no. 61.

[175] Ibid., no. 56.

[176] Ibid., no. 53.

[177] Ibid. no. 65.

[178] Pope Paul VI, op. cit., nos. 15, 30.

[179] Ibid., no. 25.

[180] art. cit. (note 45, part two), p. 11.

[181] Cf. ibid., no. 246.

[182] "Le Verbe éternel, la Sagesse Éternelle, ayant résolu, dans le grand conseil de la sainte Trinité, de se faire homme pour réparer l'homme perdu, fit connaître à Adam, comme il est croyable, et promit aux anciens Patriarches, comme la sainte Écriture le marque, qu'il se ferait homme pour racheter le monde" (Sagesse, no. 104).

[183] "Consequently, when Christ came into the world, he said, 'Sacrifices and offerings thou hast not desired, but a body hast thou prepared for me; in burnt offerings and sin offerings thou hast taken no pleasure. Then I said, 'Lo, I have come to do thy will, O God,' as it is written of me in the roll of the book.' When he said above, 'Thou hast neither desired nor taken pleasure in sacrifices and

sin offerings' (these are offered according to the law), then he added, 'Lo, I have come to do thy will.' He abolishes the first in order to establish the second. And by that will we have been sanctified through the offering of the body of Jesus Christ once for all."

[184] "Mon coeur est prêt, mon Dieu, mon Père, à faire votre volonté, içi dans le sein de ma Mère, je m'y soumets en vérité. Je vous adore et je vous aime, Me voilà, disposez de moi. Je place au milieu de moi-même et votre croix et votre loi. Vous me faites voir à cette heure qu'il faut que j'embrasse la croix et qu'il faut même que j'y meure, je le veux, mon Dieu, c'est mon choix" (*Cantiques*, p. 113).

[185] "C'est en ce mystère qu'il a opéré tous les mystères de sa vie qui ont suivi, par l'acceptation qu'il en fit: *Jesus ingrediens mundum dicit: Ecce venio ut faciam Deus, voluntatem tuam;* et par consequent, que ce mystère est un abrégé de tous les mystères, qui renferme la volonté et la grace de tous" (*V.Dév.*, no. 248).

[186] Cf. *Secret du Rosaire*, p. 50.

[187] Pope Paul VI, *op. cit.*, no. 6.

[188] *Ibid.*, no. 46.

[189] "Leurs cris, leurs prières, et leurs sacrifices n'avaient pas assez de force pour attirer la Sagesse Éternelle... leurs sacrifices de leurs coeurs... n'étaient pas d'un assez grand prix pour mériter cette grâce des grâces" (*Sagesse*, no. 104).

[190] "Il ne s'est trouvé que Marie qui par la sublimité de sa vertu a atteint jusqu'au trône de la Divinité et a mérité ce trésor infini" (*V.Dév.*, no. 16).

[191] "Il n'y a eu que Marie qui l'ait mérité et trouvé grace devant Dieu par la force de ses prières et la hauteur de ses vertus" (*ibid.*, 1. c.).

[192] "La Sagesse Éternelle désirait se faire homme en elle pourvu qu'elle donnât son consentement" (*Sagesse*, no. 107).

[193] "Cette salutation a été présentée pour terminer l'affaire la plus grande et la plus importante du monde, l'Incarnation du Verbe Éternel" (*Secret du Rosaire*, p. 49).

[194] Cf. *Lettre aux amis de la croix*, no. 53. Nowhere does Saint Louis explicitly treat of Mary's knowledge at the Annunciation; yet that Our Lady did understand in some way that the event was redemptive in character is clearly implied in his other texts cited.

[195] Pope Paul VI, *op. cit.*, no. 6.

[196] *Ibid.*, no. 28.

[197] *Ibid.*, no. 37.

[198] *Ibid.*, no. 6.

[199] *Dogmatic Constitution on the Church*, in *op. cit.*, no. 62.

[200] *Ibid.*, no. 56.

[201] *Behold Your Mother*, no. 28.

[202] "Leurs coeurs, unis très fortement par des liens intimes, s'offrent tous deux, conjointement, pour être deux victimes, pour arrêter le châtiment que méritent nos crimes" (*Cantiques*, p. 154).

[203] "Dans ce mystère, les élus ont reçu leur naissance. Marie unie avec Jésus les ont pris par avance pour avoir part à leurs vertus, leur gloire et leur puissance" (*ibid.*, 1. c.).

[204] "C'est en ce mystère que Jésus, de concert avec Marie...a choisi tous les élus" (*V.Dév.*, no. 248).

[205] Cf. *Secret du Rosaire*, p. 50; *Cantiques*, p. 40: "Vous nous donnez la vie, puisque vous brisez nos liens"; the quotes which follow support this point. It is also interesting to note that Saint Louis had also copied in his notebook these words of Poiré: "Elle a travaillé à mettre au monde ses enfants spirituels particulièrement sur le Calvaire, où Notre Seigneur comme père les mettait au monde et Marie comme mère" (*Cahier de Notes*, p. 91); cf. F. Poiré, *op. cit.*, pp. 12 ff.

[206] "Il a glorifié son indépendance et sa majesté à dépendre de cette aimable Vierge dans sa conception, en sa naissance, en sa présentation au temple, en sa vie cachée de trente ans, jusqu'à sa mort, où elle devait assister, pour ne faire avec elle qu'un même sacrifice et pour être immolé par son consentement au Père éternel, comme autrefois Isaac par le consentement d'Abraham à la volonté de Dieu" (*V.Dév.*, no. 18).

[207] "C'est elle qui l'a allaité, nourri, entretenu, élevé et sacrifié pour nous" (*ibid.*, 1. c.).

[208] *Dogmatic Constitution on the Church*, in *op. cit.*, no. 57.

[209] *Ibid.*, no. 58; text repeated by Pope Paul VI, *op. cit.*, no. 20.

[210] *Ibid.*, no. 61.

[211] Pope Paul VI, *op. cit.*, 28; cf. *ibid.*, no. 20, no. 57.

[212] *Ibid.*, no. 37

[213] *Behold Your Mother*, no. 120; cf. *ibid.*, no. 18.

[214] Cf. note 45, part two.

[215] Cf. *Cantiques*, p. 152.

[216] Cf. G. Roschini, *La corredentrice degli uomini secondo il beato di Montfort*, in *Regina dei Cuori*, Vol. XXVII (1940), p. 24; J. Hermans, *op. cit.*, pp. 138 ff.

[217] "Pécheurs, nous faisons par nos crimes de Marie et Jésus, deux très innocentes victimes" (*Cantiques*, p. 153).

[218] Cf. *ibid.*, p. 154.

[219] "Une illustre conquête de Jésus-Christ crucifié sur le Calvaire en union de sa sainte Mère" (*Lettre aux amis de la croix*, no. 4).

[220] *Cantiques*, p. 40.

[221] Cf. Pius XII, *Mystici corporis*, "ob novum etiam doloris gloriaeque titulum, ejus membrorum omnium mater." (*AAS*, XXXV

(1943), pp. 247-248).

[222] "Elle a donné par son Fils et la grace et la gloire, la vie aux morts..." (*Cantiques*, p. 181).

[223] "Vous nous donnez la vie à tous en nous donnant le fruit de vie" (*ibid.*, p. 30).

[224] "Vous nous donnez la vie en nous donnant cet aimable Sauveur" (*ibid.*, p. 43).

[225] "C'est elle qui a donné l'être et la vie à l'Auteur de toute grace, et, à cause de cela, elle est appelée la Mère de la grâce, Mater gratiae" (*Secret*, no. 8).

[226] "Si Jésus-Christ le chef des hommes est né en elle, les prédestinés qui sont les membres de ce chef, doivent aussi naître en elle par une suite nécessaire. Une même mère ne met pas au monde la tête ou le chef sans les membres, ni les membres sans la tête: autrement ce serait un monstre de nature; de même, dans l'ordre de la grâce, le chef et les membres naissent d'une même mère; et si un membre du corps mystique de Jésus-Christ, c'est-à-dire un prédestiné, naissait d'une autre mère que Marie qui a produit le chef, ce ne serait pas un prédestiné ni un membre de Jésus-Christ, mais un monstre dans l'ordre de la grâce" (*V. Dév.*, no. 32).

[227] "Puisque Marie a formé le Chef des prédestinés qui est Jésus-Christ, c'est elle aussi de former les membres de ce Chef, qui sont les vrais chrétiens; car une mère ne forme pas le chef sans les membres, ni les membres sans le chef" (*Secret*, no. 12).

[228] "Remarquez que non seulement Marie est la mère de Jésus, le chef de tous les élus, mais encore qu'elle est (la Mère) de tous ses membres; en sorte que c'est elle qui les engendre, les porte dans son sein, et les met au monde de la gloire, par les grâces de Dieu qu'elle leur communique" (*Sagesse*, no. 213).

[229] Cf. *V.Dév.*, nos. 17, 21; *Prière pour Missionnaires*, pp. 88-89.

[230] Cf. J. Zimara in his review of R. Bernard's book, *Le mystère de Marie*, in *Divus Thomas*, Freiburg, (Marz 1935), pp. 104 ff.

[231] Cf. E. Mura, *Le corps mystique du Christ*, Vol. II (Paris, 1937), p. 147.

[232] Cf. E. Mura, *op. cit.*, Vol. II, p. 143, note. Pius X himself declared that he relied upon Montfort's *True Devotion* in composing his encyclical *Ad diem illum*. Cf. *Regina dei Cuori*, Vol. I (1913), p. 124; L. Locatelli, S.M.M., *Il pensiero mariano de Beato Pio X*, in *Madre e Regina*, Vol. V (June 1951), p. 145.

[233] Pius X, *Ad diem illum*, ASS, XXXVI (1904-1905), p. 452.

[234] Cf. Pius XII, *Mystici Corporis*, AAS, XXXV (1943), pp. 247-248; N.C.W.C. translation, no. 107. Pope Pius XII uses the term *Genetrix*, for Mary's spiritual motherhood.

[235] Pope Paul VI, *op. cit.*, no. 11.

[236] *Behold Your Mother,* no 70.

[237] *Ibid.,* no. 71.

[238] *Dogmatic Constitution on the Church,* in *op. cit.,* no. 53.

[239] Romans 12:4-5; cf. Eph. 5:30; Coloss. 1:18.

[240] *S.Th.* III, q. 49, a. 1, corp.; cf. also III, q. 48, a. 2 ad 1.

[241] Pius XII, *Mystici Corporis, AAS,* XXXV (1943), p. 226.

[242] Cf. *ibid.,* 1. c.

[243] E. Mura, *op. cit.,* Vol. I, (Paris, 1936), pp. 253-254.

[244] E. Mura distinguishes seven various principles of unity in the Mystical Body, then declares: "Ce principe de causalité efficiente qui appartient au Christ notre Chef est en réalité... le premier des principes qui interviennent dans la constitution du Corps mystique de Jésus... C'est avant tout la grâce capitale qui constitue la Personne mystique du Christ plénier" (*op. cit.,* Vol. I, p. 256).

[245] That Christ possessed capital grace at the Incarnation is also stated by Pius XII, *Mystici corporis, AAS,* XXXV (1943) p. 247; however, it may be said that He possesses this Headship in the full sense of the term at Calvary (*ibid.,* p. 206). This is also expressed equivalently by C. Dillenschneider *Pour une Corredemption Mariale bien Comprise,* (Rome, 1949), p. 94: "notre incorporation objective au Christ Chef, Sauveur des hommes, inaugurée à l'Incarnation, s'est poursuivie par une sorte de continuité intrinsèque et s'est consommée sur le Calvaire." It is difficult to see, therefore, how some authors claim that the spiritual maternity cannot be deduced from the fact that Mary gave birth to the Head of the Mystical Body because Our Lord possessed at the Incarnation what they term mere 'juridical' Headship. (cf. Gregorio de Jesus Crucificado, *art cit.,* p. 132; followed closely by W. Sebastian, *The nature of Mary's spiritual maternity,* in *Marian Studies,* Vol. III (1952), p. 26).

[246] The subject of generation is not a nature but a person, according to the axiom, *"actiones et passiones sunt suppositorum."* The Suppositum generated by Mary is the Word of God; she is, therefore, the Mother of God, according to His human nature.

[247] Cf. *S.Th.,* III, q. 8, a. 1.

[248] *V.Dév.,* no. 16.

[249] *Sagesse,* no. 107.

[250] *S.Th.,* III, q. 30, a. 1.

[251] "(La Divine Sagesse) désirait se faire homme en elle, pourvu qu'elle y donnât son consentement" (*Sagesse,* no. 107). Cf. *V.Dév.,* no. 49.

[252] *Dogmatic Constitution on the Church,* in *op.cit.,* no. 56.

[253] "Le Verbe s'est fait chair; la Saggesse éternelle s'est incarnée. Dieu est devenu homme, sans cesser d'être Dieu; cet Homme-Dieu s'appelle Jésus-Christ, c'est-à-dire, Sauveur" (*Sagesse,* no.

108).

254 *V.Dév.*, no. 16.

255 *Ibid.*, no. 49.

256 *Cantiques*, p. 180.

257 Pope Paul VI, *op. cit.*, no. 6. Cf. the strong statement of Pope Paul in his address *Mary, Exemplary Model and Ideal Figure of the Church* in *Osservatore Romano* (English edition), Dec. 18, 1975, p. 6: "Mary represented in herself the figure of the Holy Church. A model, a specimen, an ideal figure of the Church; is that enough? The theological truth goes further and enters the frontiers of that subordinate causality which in the divine plan of salvation inseparably associates the creature, Mary, the Handmaid of the 'Fiat,' with the mystery of the Incarnation and makes her, Saint Irenaeus writes, 'a cause of this salvation for herself and for the whole of mankind' (*Adv. haereses, III, 22, 4*)."

258 *Behold Your Mother*, no. 18.

259 *Dogmatic Constitution on the Church*, in *op. cit.*, no. 56.

260 Cf. note 45, part two.

261 K. Rahner, *Mary Mother of the Lord. Theological Meditations*, (New York, 1964), pp. 100-101.

262 *Ibid.*, p. 105.

263 "Les prédestinés sont tous enfermés dans le sein de Marie et ... ils ne viennent au jour que lorsque cette bonne Mère les enfante à la vie éternelle" (*Secret*, no. 14).

264 "vrais enfants de Marie ... qui soient engendrés et conçus par sa charité, portés dans son sein, attachés à ses mamelles, nourris de son lait, élevés par ses soins, soutenus de ses bras et enrichis de ses grâces" (*Prière pour Missionnaires*, p. 86).

265 "Mon sein vous donne le jour, c'est moi qui vous engendre" (*Cantiques*, p. 172).

266 Cf. M. Phillipon, *art. cit.*, p. 66: "Grignion de Montfort, l'incomparable docteur de la maternité spirituelle de Marie."

267 Cf. *AAS*, Vol. 39 (1947), p. 331.

268 *V.Dév.*, no. 118.

269 *Translator's Preface*, found in *The True Devotion*, pp. xvii-xviii.

270 Cf. Introduction, note 26, supra.

271 R. Bernard, *Le Mystère de Marie*, (Paris, 1933), p. 9.

BIBLIOGRAPHY

I. *Sources: The Writings of Saint Louis de Montfort*

1. *L'Amour de la Sagesse Éternelle*, Édition Type, Librairie Mariale, Pontchâteau, 1929.
   The Love of Eternal Wisdom, Montfort Publications, Bay Shore, N.Y. 1960.
2. *Cahier de Notes*. Excerpts published in *Oeuvres complètes* de Saint Louis-Marie Grignion de Montfort, Paris, 1966.
   Not published in English.
3. *Cahier de Sermons*. Excerpts published in *Oeuvres complètes*.
   Not published in English.
4. *Cantiques du Bienheureux de Montfort*, Edition Type, Librairie Mariale, Pontchâteau, 1929.
   Not published in English.
5. *Pour bien Mourir*, Saint Laurent-sur-Sèvre, Vendée, 1927.
   Preparation For a Happy Death, Bay Shore, N.Y. 1954.
6. *Lettre Circulaire du Bienheureux Louis-Marie Grignion de Montfort aux Amis de la Croix*, Les Traditions Françaises, Tourcoing, 1947.
   Friends Of The Cross, Montfort Publications, Bay Shore, N.Y. 1972.
7. *Lettres du Bienheureux de Montfort*, Saint Laurent-sur-Sèvre, Vendée, 1928.
   Not published in English.
8. *Prière pour demander des Missionnaires pour la Compagnie de Marie. Règle de la Compagnie de Marie.*
   Prayer For Missionaries, Montfort Publications, Bay Shore, N.Y. 1958.
   Allocution aux Associés de la Compagnie de Marie.
   All found in the *Vade-Mecum du Montfortain*, Mame, Tours, 1932; The *Prière* and *Allocution* are also found in the edition of *Le Secret de Marie* mentioned below. Neither the *Rule of the Company of Mary* nor the *Allocution to the Members of the Company of Mary* are published in English.

9. *Règle des Filles de la Sagesse.* Imprimerie Aimé Barbier, Poitiers, 1818.
Not published in English.

10. *Le Secret Admirable du Très Saint Rosaire pour se convertir et se sauver,* Oudin, Paris, 1912.
The Secret Of The Rosary, Montfort Publications, Bay Shore, N.Y. 1974.

11. *Le Secret de Marie,* Lescuyer & Fils, Lyon, 1956.
The Secret of Mary Montfort Publications, Bay Shore, N.Y. 1975.

12. *Traité de la Vraie Dévotion à la Très Sainte Vierge,* Secrétariat de Marie Médiatrice, Louvain, 1947; *Reproduction Photographique du Manuscrit,* Rome, 1942.
True Devotion To Mary, Montfort Publications, Bay Shore, N.Y. 1975.

13. *Oeuvres complètes de Saint Louis Marie-Grignion de Montfort,* Éditions du Seuil, Paris, 1966. Cf. note 41 of Introduction.

✠   ✠   ✠

II. *Principal Works*

ABBOTT, W., AND GALLAGHER, J., (ed.). *The Documents of Vatican II,* America Press, New York, 1966.

AGUDELO, F., *Naturaleza de la esclavitud mariana segun el Padre Bartolome de los Rios y San Luís Maria de Montfort,* Bogotá, 1958.

BERNARD., R.P., *Le Mystère de Marie, Les Origines et Les Grands Actes de la Maternité de Grâce de la Sainte Vierge,* Desclée de Brouwer, Paris, 1933.

BLAIN, J. B., *Abrégé de la vie de Louis-Marie Grignion de Montfort. Texte établi, présenté et annoté par Louis Pérouas,* Centre International Montfortain, Roma, 1973.

BOUDON, H. M., *Dieu Seul ou Le Saint Esclavage de l'Admirable Mère de Dieu. Oeuvres complètes de Boudon,* édition Migne, Paris, 1857.

BRAUN, F. M., *La Mère des Fideles. Essai de Théologie Johannique,* Casterman, Tournai, 1954.

BROWN, R., FITZMYER, J., MURPHY, R., *The Jerome Biblical Commentary,* Prentice-Hall, Englewood Cliffs, New Jersey, 1968.

CRASSET, J. B., *La véritable dévotion envers la Sainte Vierge établie et défendue,* Paris, 1679.

D'ARGENTAN, L. F., *Conférences Théologiques et Spirituelles sur les grandeurs de la très Sainte Vierge Marie, Mère de Dieu,* Paris, 1687.

DAYET, R. P., *La Parfaite Dévotion á Marie*, Les Editions Francaises, 1946.

DE BERULLE, CARDINAL, *Oeuvres complètes*, édition Migne, Paris, 1856.

DE BERULLE-GIBIEUF-OLIER, as found in Molien, A., *La Vierge Mère de Dieu, Les Meilleurs Textes de l'Ecole Française, De Bérulle-Gibieuf-Olier, ou Les Grandeurs de Marie*, Desclée de Brouwer, Paris, 1940.

DE LA BROISE ET BAINVEL, *Marie, Mère de Grâce, Étude Doctrinale*, Beauchesne, Paris, 1921.

DILLENSCHNEIDER, C., *La Mariologie de S. Alphonse de Liguori, Son Influence sur le Renouveau des doctrines mariales et de la piété catholique, après la tourmente du protestantisme et du jansénisme*, Studia Friburgensia, Fribourg (Suisse), 1931.

————*La Mariologie de S. Alphonse de Liguori, Source et Synthèse Doctrinale*, Studia Friburgensia, Fribourg (Suisse), 1934.

————*Marie au Service de notre rédemption, le mérite médiateur de la nouvelle Éve dans l'économie rédemptrice*, Bureau du Perpétuel Secours, Haguneau, 1947.

————*Le Principe Premier d'une théologie Mariale organique*, Éditions Alsatia, Paris, 1955.

FEUILLET, A., *Jésus et sa mère d'après les recits Lucaniens de l'enfance et d'après saint Jean*, Gabalda, Paris, 1974.

GARCES, G., *Mater Corredemptrix, seu de possibili illatione a spirituali maternitate B.M.V. ad formalem ejus corredemptionem*, Marietti, Romae, MCMXL.

GARRIGOU-LAGRANGE, R., *La Mère du Sauveur et notre vie intérieure*, Les Éditions de l'Abeille, Lyon, 1941.

GRANDET, M., *La vie de Messire Louis-Marie Grignion de Montfort, Prêtre Missionnaire Apostolique, composée par un prêtre du clergé*, Verger, Nantes, 1724.

GUINDON, H., *Marie de Vatican II*, Beauchesne, Paris, 1971.

HERMANS, J. M., *Maria's Middelaarschap volgens de leer van de Heilige Louis-Marie Grignion de Montfort*, N.V. Lecturis, Eindhoven, 1947.

HOFFER, P., *La dévotion à Marie au déclin du XVIIe siècle, Les Avis Salutaires de la B.V.M.*, Edition du Cerf, Paris, 1938.

HUGON, E., *La Mère de grâce*, Lethielleux, Paris, 1904.

KEUPPENS, J., *Mariologiae Compendium*, Louvain, 1947.

LAURENTIN, R., *Court Traité de théologie Mariale*, Lethielleux, Paris, 1953.

————*La Vierge au Concile*, Paris, 1965.

LE CROM, L., *Un Apôtre Marial, Saint Louis-Marie Grignion de Montfort*, Les Éditions Françaises, Tourcoing, 1946.

LENNERZ, H., *De Beata Virgine, Tractatus Dogmaticus,* Apud Aedes Universitatis Gregorianae, Romae, 1957.

LHOUMEAU, A., *La Vie Spirituelle á l'école de saint Louis-Marie Grignion de Montfort,* Beyaert, Bruges, 1954.

MANTEAU-BONAMY, *La Vierge et le Saint Esprit,* Paris, 1971.

MARVULLI, L., *Maria Madre del Cristo Mistico. La Maternità di Maria nel suo concetto theologico integrale,* Pontificia Facoltà Theologica O.F.M. Conv., Romae, 1948.

MERKELBACH, B., *Mariologia,* Desclée de Brouwer, Paris, 1939.

MURA, E., *Le Corps mystique du Christ. Sa Nature et Sa Vie, synthese de théologie dogmatique, ascétique et mystique,* 2 Vols., André Blot, Paris, 1936-1937.

NATIONAL CONFERENCE OF CATHOLIC BISHOPS, *Behold Your Mother, Woman of Faith. A Pastoral Letter on the Blessed Virgin Mary,* U.S. Catholic Conference, Washington, 1973.

NEUBERT, E., *Marie dans le dogme,* Édition Spes, Paris, 1953.

OLIER, J. J., *Oeuvres complètes,* Édition Migne, Paris, 1856.

PAUL VI, *Apostolic Exhortation, Signum Magnum, AAS,* 59 (1967).

————*Address in the Vatican Basilica to the Fathers of the Council, 21 November, 1964, AAS,* 56 (1964).

————*Apostolic Exhortation, Marialis Cultus,* February 2, 1974, U.S. Catholic Conference, Washington, 1974.

PIUS X, *Ad diem illum, ASS,* XXXVI (1904-1905).

PIUS XII, *Mystici corporis, AAS,* 35 (1943).

PEROUAS, L., *Ce que croyait Grignion de Montfort et comment il a vecu sa foi,* Mame, Paris, 1973.

PLESSIS, P., *Manuale Mariologiae Dogmaticae,* Librairie Mariale, Pontchâteau, 1942.

————*Commentaire du Traité de la Vraie Dévotion à la Sainte Vierge du Bx. Grignion de Montfort,* Librairie Mariale, Pontchateau, 1943.

POHLE-PREUSS, *Mariology, A Dogmatic Treatise on the Blessed Virgin Mother of God,* Herder, St. Louis, 1922.

POIRÉ, F., *La Triple Couronne de la Bienheureuse Vierge Mère de Dieu,* Paris, 1639.

POUPON, P., *Le Poème de la parfaite consécration à Marie suivant Saint Louis-Marie Grignion de Montfort et les spirituels de son temps. Sources et doctrine,* Librairie du Sacré Coeur, Lyon, 1947.

————*A Jésus par Marie, La parfaite consécration à Marie selon Saint Louis-Marie Grignion de Montfort,* Librairie du Sacré Coeur, 1948.

RAHNER, H., *Maria und die Kirche,* Innsbruck, 1951.
Our Lady and the Church, New York, 1961.

RAHNER, K., *Maria Mutter des Herrn*, Freiburg, 1956.
  Mary Mother of the Lord. Theological Meditations, Herder
  and Herder, 1963.
———(ed.). *Encyclopedia of Theology, The Concise Sacramentum
  Mundi*, Seabury Press, New York, 1975.
ROSCHINI, G., *Mariologia*, 4 Vols., Angelus Belardetti, Romae, 1947.
SCHEEBEN, M. J., *Mariology*, 2 Vols., Herder, St. Louis, 1946.
SCHILLEBEECKX, E., *Maria Moeder van de verlossing*, Bilthoven,
  1963.
  Mary Mother of the Redemption, Sheed & Ward, New York,
  1964.
———*The Understanding of Faith, Interpretation and criticism*,
  The Seabury Press, New York, 1974.
TERRIEN, J. B., *La Mère de Dieu et la Mère des Hommes, d'après
  les Pères et la Théologie*, 4 Vols., Lethielleux, Paris, 1902.
THEORET, E., *La Mediation Mariale dans l'École Française*, Vrin,
  Paris, 1940.
THOMAS (S), *Summa Theologica, I, II, III*, Marietti, Romae, 1952.
———*Commentarium in I, III, IV, Sent.*, in *Opera Omnia*, Vives,
  Paris, 1880.
VORGRIMLER, H., (ed.), *Commentary on the Documents of Vatican II*,
  Vol. I, Herder and Herder, 1967.

✠   ✠   ✠

III. *Principal Articles*

BARTOLOMEI, T., *La Maternità spirituale di Maria, sua realtà e
  svilluppo, sua natura ed estensione*, in *Divus Thomas* (Pl.),
  Vol. LV (1952), pp. 63-86.
BOVER, J., *"Mulier, ecce filius tuus"*: *Spiritualis et universalis B.M.
  Maternitas ex verbis Christi morientis demonstrata*, in *Verbum Domini*, Vol. IV (1924), pp. 225-231.
———*La Maternidad espiritual de Maria en los Padres Griegos*,
  in *Estudios Marianos*, Vol. VII (1948), pp. 91-103.
CARROLL, E. R., *Mariology*, in *Chicago Studies*, Vol. 12 (Fall, 1973),
  pp. 295-303.
———*A Survey of Recent Mariology*, in *Marian Studies*, yearly
  issue.
CAZELLES, H., *L'Esprit Saint et l'Incarnation dans le developpement
  de la revelation biblique*, in *Bulletin de la Societé Françaises
  d'Etudes Mariales*, Vol. 26 (1969), pp. 9-20.
DAYET, R. P., *La Maternité spirituelle, fondement de la parfaite dévotion*, in *Revue des Prêtres de Marie*, Vol. XXI (1934), pp.
  129 ff.

————*Montfort et la maternité spirituelle,* in *ibid.,* Vol. XXXV (1949), pp. 65 ff., 129 ff., 161 ff.

DE FIORES, S., *La devozione mariana del Montfort nel contesto della polemica degli "Avvisi Salutari" di Widenfeld,* in *Marianum,* 36 (1974), pp. 40-69.

————*St. Louis Mary de Montfort's spiritual intinerary in the Period prior to his Ordination, June 5, 1700.* Marian Library Studies, Vol. VI, 1974. Dayton, Ohio. (in Italian)

DE GOEDT, M., *Bases bibliques de la maternité spirituelle,* in *Bulletin de la Societé Française d'Études Mariales,* Vol. 16 (1959), pp. 18 ff.

DEVY, V., *La Royauté universelle de Notre Dame, Marie Reine des Coeurs,* in *Nouvelle Revue Mariale,* No. 8 (1956), pp. 18 ff.

DUBLANCHY, E., art. *Marie,* in *Dictionnaire de Théologie Catholique,* Tome IX, 2ième partie, Letouzey et Ané (Paris, 1927), col. 2339 ff.

FRANZI, P., *Maternità spirituale intesa dal Montfort,* in *Madre e Regina,* Vol. XI (1957), pp. 27-29; pp. 53-55; pp. 85-87.

FREHEN, H., *De Maternitate Spirituali B.M.V. ad mentem S. Ludovici Mariae de Montfort,* in *Alma Socia Christi,* Vol. VIII (1953), pp. 27-44.

GAFFNEY, P., *The Holy Slavery of Love,* in *Mariology,* ed. J. B. Carol, Vol. 3, (Milwaukee, 1961), pp. 143-161.

GARRETA, J., *La Maternidad espiritual de Maria en los Padres Latinos,* in *Estudios Marianos,* Vol. VII (1948), pp. 105-118.

GEBHARD, H. M., *Commentaire du Traité de la Vraie Dévotion à la Sainte Vierge,* in *Revue des Prêtres de Marie,* Janv., 1922-Sept. Oct., 1944.

GEENEN, G., *Marie Notre Mère, Esquisse historique et évolution doctrinale,* in *Marianum,* Vol. X (1948), pp. 337-352.

GUILIANI, L., *La cooperazione di Maria SS., alla nostra redenzione e S. Luigi Maria Grignion da Montfort,* in *Marianum,* Vol. X (1948), pp. 31-65.

GREGORIO DE JESUS CRUCIFICADO, *Naturaleza de la Maternidad espiritual de Maria,* in *Estudios Marianos,* Vol. VII (1948), pp. 121-143.

GUINDON, H., *La coopération de la très-sainte Vierge à l'acquisition et à la distribution de la grâce selon Saint Louis-Marie de Montfort,* in *Alma Socia Christi,* Vol. VIII (1953), pp. 66-95.

HUPPERTS, J. M., *Saint Louis-Marie de Montfort et sa spiritualité mariale,* in *Maria. Etudes sur la Sainte Vierge,* ed. H. du Manoir, Vol. III (Paris, 1954), pp. 251-274.

HUMENAY, R., *The Place of Mary in Luke: A Look at Modern Biblical Criticism,* in *The American Ecclesiastical Review,*

(1974), pp. 291-303.

LAURENTIN, R., *Bulletin sur la Vierge Marie* in *Revue des Sciences Philosophiques et Théologiques*. This excellent review of Mariological literature appears in every other issue.

——*Foi et mythe en théologie Mariale*, in *Nouvelle Revue Théologique*, 89 (1967), pp. 26-42.

LLAMERA, M., *La Maternidad espiritual de Maria*, in *Estudios Marianos*, Vol. III (1944), pp. 67-162.

MAY, E., *The Scriptural Basis for Mary's Spiritual Maternity*, in *Marian Studies*, Vol. III (1952), pp. 111-142.

MURA, E., *De leer over het mystieke lichaam in de mariologie van de H. Louis-Marie de Montfort*, in *Montfort, zijn geestelijke vorming en levenswerk*, Bijdragen (1947), pp. 147-176.

NICHOLAS, J., *Synthèse mariale*, in *Maria: Études sur la Sainte Vierge*, ed. du Manoir, Vol. I (Paris, 1949), pp. 707-744.

O'CONNOR, W., *The Spiritual Maternity of Our Lady in Tradition*, in *Marian Studies*, Vol. III (1952), pp. 142-174.

OGER, P., *Intorno ad un passo discusso del tratto della vera devozione di S.L.M. di Montfort*, in *Marianum*, Vol. X (1948), pp. 364 ff.

PHILIPS, G., *Le Saint Esprit et Marie dans l'Église. Vatican II et prospective du probléme*, in *Bulletin Français d'Etudes Mariales*, Vol. 25 (1968), pp. 7-37.

——*La Vierge au Concile du Vatican et l'Avenir de la Mariologie*, in *Maria. Études sur la Sainte Vierge*, ed. H. du Manoir, Vol. VIII (Paris, 1971), pp. 43-88. (Includes excellent bibliography on Mary and the Council).

PHILLIPON, M., *Maternité spirituelle de Marie et de l'église*, in *Bulletin de la Societé Française d'Etudes Mariales*, Vol. X (1952), pp. 63-86.

DE LA POTTERIE, I., *La parole de Jesus, Voiçi ta mère et l'accueil du disciple*, Jn 19:27b, in *Marianum*, 36 (1974), pp. 1-39.

RAHNER, K., *The Immaculate Conception*, in *Theological Investigations*, Vol. I (Baltimore, 1961), pp. 201-213.

SALGADO, J. M., *La maternité spirituelle et la Très Sainte Vierge Marie. Bilan Actuel*, in *Divinitas*, 16 (1972), pp. 17-102.

SCHMAUS, M., *Mariology*, in *Sacramentum Mundi, An Encyclopedia of Theology*, Vol. 3, Herder and Herder (New York, 1969), pp. 376-390. Abbreviated article found in *Encyclopedia of Theology, The Concise Sacramentum Mundi*, ed. K. Rahner, Seabury Press, (New York, 1975), pp. 893-904.

SEBASTIAN, W., *The Nature of Mary's Spiritual Maternity*, in *Marian Studies*, Vol. III (1952), pp. 14-34. *Mary's Spiritual Maternity*, in *Mariology*, ed. J. B. Carol, Vol. 2 (Milwaukee, 1957), pp. 325-376.

SEMMELROTH, O., *Dogmatic Constitution on the Church, Chapter VIII, The Role of the Blessed Virgin Mary, Mother of God, in the Mystery of Christ and the Church,* in *Commentary on the Documents of Vatican II,* Vol. I, ed. H. Vorgrimler, Herder and Herder, 1967, pp. 285-296.

SETZER, F., *The Spiritual Maternity and Saint Louis Mary de Montfort,* in *Marian Studies,* Vol. III (1952), pp. 197-207.

SHEA, G. W., *The Teaching of the Magisterium on Mary's Spiritual Maternity,* in *ibid.,* pp. 35-110.

————*Outline History of Mariology in the Middle Ages and Modern Times,* in *Mariology,* ed. J. B. Carol, Vol. I (Milwaukee, 1955), pp. 281-327

Father Patrick Gaffney, a member of the Montfort Missionaries, was born in New York City, in 1928. After his ordination in 1954, he pursued his theological studies at the Pontifical University of Saint Thomas, in Rome, where he completed his doctoral work *summa cum laude,* in 1957. Father Gaffney taught theology at St. Louis de Montfort Seminary, Litchfield, Conn., where he held the post of rector for four years. He also taught at the Catholic University of Ponce, Puerto Rico, and the Inter-American University (Presbyterian) at San German, Puerto Rico, before being named Chairman of the Theology Department of Saint Louis University, St. Louis, Mo. Having completed seven years as Chairman of the Department, Father is currently Professor of Theological Studies at St. Louis University. Father Gaffney is also Associate Editor of *Horizons,* the theological journal of the College Theology Society and Vice-Chairman of the Theology Commission of the Archdiocese of Saint Louis. Born of deaf parents, Father Gaffney is adept in the sign language. Father has travelled extensively throughout Europe and the Holy Land as well as the length and breadth of America giving conferences to priests and Religious.

MP

MONTFORT PUBLICATIONS